The history of the Jews
From the war with Rome to the present time
Part II

by

H. C. Adams

Double9
BOOKS

The history of the Jews

From the war with Rome to the present time
Part II
by H. C. Adams

ISBN: 978-93-62209-48-1

Published by

DOUBLE 9 BOOKS

2/13-B, Ansari Road
Daryaganj, New Delhi – 110002
info@double9books.com
www.double9books.com
Tel. 011-40042856

This book is under public domain

ABOUT THE AUTHOR

Reverend Henry Cadwallader Adams (1817-1899) changed into a distinguished English cleric, schoolmaster, and renowned author of kid's novels at some point of the nineteenth century. Born on November four, 1817, he got here from a splendid lineage because the grandson of Simon Adams from Ansty Hall in Warwickshire. Adams acquired his schooling at prestigious institutions, together with Westminster School and Winchester College. Subsequently, he continued his educational journey at Balliol College in 1835 and Magdalen College, Oxford in 1836. His academic interests culminated in becoming a fellow of Magdalen in 1843, reflecting his scholarly achievements. Notably, Adams served as a Commoner Tutor at Winchester College, wherein he contributed to the schooling of young minds. His dedication to schooling and spirituality led to his appointment as the chaplain of Bromley College in 1855. Bromley College turned into an almshouse devoted to the aid of widows of priests, wherein Adams persevered his carrier to the community and the church. In addition to his clerical obligations, Adams made a lasting effect on children's literature together with his creative and engaging novels. His existence's work remains a testament to his multifaceted contributions as an educator, cleric, and writer at some point of the Victorian technology. Henry Cadwallader Adams exceeded away on October 17, 1899, leaving behind a legacy of literary and academic accomplishments.

CONTENTS

PREFACE

The reader will understand that this work does not profess to be anything more than a popular history, with just so much reference to Jewish learning and controversy as may be necessary to a due comprehension of the facts related, and the character of the people treated of. But such references will not, for various reasons, be frequent. Of the vast accumulations of Jewish literature, the most valuable portions are the Commentaries of their doctors on Scripture, and their contributions to grammar, mathematics, and physical science. With these, however, the writer of history has but little concern. The abstruse and intricate speculations of the Rabbins, the subtleties of the Cabbalists, the wild fancies—or what, at all events, the sober Western intellect accounts such—of the Talmuds, the Sepher-Yetzira, and the Zohar, might absorb whole years of study, but would yield the historian only a barren return for the labour. The poetry of the Hebrews is said to be plaintive and touching, but too exclusively national to have interest for any but Jews. Their ancient historians, again, overlay their narratives with exaggeration and fable to such an extent that their statements cannot be received without the greatest caution. It is mainly from writers belonging to other races that we must derive our record of the strange and varied fortunes of the people of Israel.

This must, of course, place them at some disadvantage. Yet there is no history so full of striking incident and mournful pathos as theirs, none which stirs such solemn questions, or imparts so profound a wisdom to those who rightly study it. As an illustration of the sad interest it awakens, the words of Leopold Zunz, one of the greatest of modern Jews, may suffice. 'If there are gradations in suffering,' he writes, 'Israel has reached its highest acme. If the long duration of sufferings, and the patience with which they are borne, ennobles a people, then the Jews may defy the high-born of any lands.' In truth, again and again, in every succeeding century of their annals, the evidences of a heroism which no persistence in severity could bend, and no pressure of persecution could break, engage the attention of the reader. Whatever may be his estimate of the worth or the demerits of the Jews, their tragic story at least commands his sympathy.

In these respects other nations, though they may not have rivalled, at least resemble, them. But there are peculiarities in their history which separate them from every other people on the earth. Foremost among these is the question—Are we still to regard them, as our fathers for so many generations regarded them, as lying under the special curse of God, a perpetual monument of His anger? Was the imprecation uttered before Pilate's tribunal (St. Matt. xxvii. 25), 'His blood be on us, and on our children!' ratified, so to speak, by Almighty God? Is the Lord's blood still upon them? Is that the true explanation of their past miseries and their present condition?

Let us consider what the guilt of the Jews, who slew the Lord, really amounted to. They do not, I believe, themselves deny that they are suffering under Divine displeasure, or that that displeasure has been occasioned by their sin. On the contrary, they hold that it is their sin that has delayed, and still delays, the coming of the Messiah. But, far from thinking that sin to have been the murder of Jesus Christ, they do not consider that their fathers were guilty in that matter at all. Their law, so they contend, requires them to put to death blasphemers and setters up of strange gods. The assertion of Jesus, 'I and My Father are one,' say they, was both blasphemy and the setting up of a strange god. They would only therefore have obeyed a Divine command if they had put Him to death. But, they add, it was not they, but the Romans, by whose sentence He died, for declaring Himself King of the Jews. This, they say, is sufficiently evident from the manner of His death by crucifixion, which was one never inflicted by Jews, and by the inscription on the cross, 'This is the King of the Jews.' It is extremely doubtful, they add, whether their fathers possessed the power of putting Him to death, but at all events they did not exercise it. The Jewish people, according to their view, had nothing to do with the matter. Some of the multitude may have imprecated the blood of Jesus on themselves and their children; but if so, the curse could only come on those few persons on whom it had been invoked. Jost and others even deny that the Sanhedrim was ever legally convened, the meeting that condemned Jesus and delated Him to Pilate being, as they hold, merely a tumultuary assembly of the enemies of Christ.

It will, of course, be answered that to charge our Lord with blasphemy and setting up of a strange god, is simply to beg the whole question at issue between Jew and Christian. Indeed, considering that the Hebrew Scriptures distinctly declare the Messiah to be God[1] (Psa. xlv. 6; Isa. vii. 14; ix. 6, etc.), according to this view of the matter, at whatever period He might come, it must be the duty of the Jews to put Him to death, as soon as He declared His true character. It might be asked—How were the Jews to know that Jesus was really what He proclaimed Himself? Our answer is, that in the fulfilment of prophecy in Him, in the exercise of His miraculous powers, and the superhuman holiness of His teaching, they had sufficient evidence that He was indeed the Christ. They had, in fact, *the* evidence of it which Divine wisdom accounted sufficient.

Again, it was doubtless by the order of a Roman magistrate that He was crucified; and it may perhaps be true that during the Roman Procuratorship the Sanhedrim had no power of pronouncing a capital sentence.[2] But it was the Jews who carried our Lord before Pilate and demanded His death. Far from being anxious to condemn Him, Pilate was most reluctant to order the execution. It was only when the dangerous insinuation of disloyalty to Cæsar was suggested that he consented to their wishes. Who can doubt that the guilt was theirs? Pilate might as well have put off the blame on the centurion who commanded the quaternion at Calvary, or he on the three soldiers who put in force the sentence. The statement again, that the Sanhedrim was not convened, is in direct contradiction to that of St. Mark (xv. 1). Nor does it appear that the Evangelist's assertion was ever called in question by contemporary writers.

There can be no reasonable doubt in the mind of any man who accepts the Gospel narrative as a true—I do not here say an inspired—history, that the Jews of that day were guilty of the blood of our Lord, and that it was a deed of the most flagrant wickedness. But it remains to be proved that they slew Him, knowing Him to be their Incarnate God, and I think that would be found extremely difficult of proof. If we are to be guided by Scripture in the matter, we shall entertain a different opinion. St. Peter said to these very men, not many weeks afterwards, 'I wot that ye did it in ignorance,' and then called upon them 'to repent, that their sin might be blotted out.'[3] Our Lord also pleaded their ignorance of the nature of the deed they were perpetrating, in their behalf.[4] Both these passages are inconsistent with the idea of an abiding and inexorable curse. Their guilt was like that of the Athenian people when they condemned Socrates to death, or of that of the Florentines, when they similarly murdered Savonarola, or again of the Romans, when they assassinated Count Rossi—like theirs, though doubtless more aggravated. The sin of rejecting the preachers of holiness, and silencing their voices in their blood, is one of the worst of which a people can be guilty, and must needs draw down the heavy wrath of the All Just; but surely not on their descendants for all after ages.

As regards the other argument advanced, no doubt the slayers of Socrates or Savonarola did not imprecate on themselves and their children the consequences of their deed, as the Jews did. But what then? The Jews at the crucifixion could have had no more power than other men to cut themselves off from repentance, much less to cut their children off from it.

The blood of Christ can cleanse men from *any* sin. This, even if it were not the plain declaration of Scripture, would be proved by St. Peter's address to them, already quoted. Even were this otherwise, what claim could these men have had to represent the Jewish people? There were, as is shown elsewhere,[5] probably some six or seven millions of Jews in the world. Of these not one half, in all likelihood, had heard of our Lord till after His death. Many never heard of Him for generations afterwards. Of the two or three millions present in the Holy Land when the crucifixion took place, not the thousandth part could have heard Pilate's protest, or the rejoinder of the crowd. On what principle is this small section to be regarded as representing the whole Jewish people, for whose words and acts it is to be held accountable? When the Cordeliers, with their frantic blasphemies, in the name of the French people disavowed God, doubtless they drew down Divine anger on all concerned; but are we to believe that the guilt of their impiety will rest on the French nation for ever? Such an idea appears to me to be alien alike to the spirit of both natural and revealed religion.

But it will, no doubt, be asked—How, then, is the strange and exceptional condition of the Jews for so many centuries to be accounted for? No careful student of God's Word will have any difficulty in answering this question. Great and enduring blessings had been promised to Abraham, 'the friend of God,' and to his posterity for his sake. These had been repeated to David, 'the man after God's own heart,' with an assurance of still greater mercies. The faithfulness of God to His promises is a thing wholly independent of lapse of time. To us, a promise given nearly 4,000 years ago may seem a thing wholly obsolete; to Him it is as fresh and binding as if it had been made yesterday. Therefore, although any other nation but that which sprung from the loins of Abraham would have been destroyed and rooted out for such a series of rebellious deeds as that which culminated in the crucifixion of the Lord, the remembrance of Abraham and David has prevented its entire destruction. We are distinctly told that this was the case at other periods of their history. When Jeroboam relapsed into idolatry, he and his whole race were cut off root and branch. But when Solomon did the same, the kingdom, though with reduced strength and splendour, was continued to his posterity. When the kingdom of Israel offended beyond endurance, it was scattered into all lands, and its nationality perished. When that of Judah was equally guilty, its dispersion was only for awhile, and then it was allowed to return and resume its national existence. A remnant of the nation was preserved for Abraham's sake, that particular remnant, for the sake of David. Such, it is most reasonable to conclude, is the true explanation of their marvellous history for the last eighteen hundred years. Their protracted existence in their present condition is indeed a miracle, but a miracle, not of wrath, but of mercy. This they are themselves quick to perceive.

But, as in the cases above alleged, the continuance of the sceptre to Solomon's descendants, and the restoration of Judah after the Captivity, did not exempt them from the penalty of their subsequent disobedience, so now the preservation of Israel through so many centuries of danger and suffering, does not annul or modify the consequences of their unbelief. Like all nations which come into contact with Christianity, but do not accept Christ, they share the benefits of His sacrifice, in the amended moral tone of the world, which is the slow growth of His teaching; but they can only gain, or to speak more correctly, regain, His favour, by taking Him as their Lord and their God.[6] They cannot rightly be said to be living under a curse, but they assuredly fail to obtain a blessing. But to this they continue persistently blind.

This is the key to their history. This is the explanation of their persistent isolation, their resolute endurance, their unconquerable self-reliance. Descendants of the special favourites of Heaven, fully persuaded that its favour has not been forfeited, but only temporarily withdrawn, this high-spirited and gifted race has ever felt that, supported by this conviction, it could, like 'the charity' of St. Paul, hope and endure all things. Races that had not sprung into existence when theirs had reached the highest point of civilization and glory, might pretend to despise them: but, to use the language which Sir Walter Scott puts into the mouth of the bard, Cadwallon, they knew that the blood which flowed in the veins of their persecutors, when compared with their own, 'was but as the puddle of the highway to the silver fountain.'[7]

Their history is sad and humiliating to read; and no less sad and humiliating to them, than to those whose ancestors trampled upon and persecuted them. It brings out into strong relief, not only the good, but also the bad points of their national character. The stubborn unbelief of generation after generation; the way in which business ability, under the pressure of injustice, developed into craft, into the power of heaping up wealth by usury, and relentless exaction of the uttermost farthing; the slow processes by which the most manifest characteristic of a Jew became that of the harsh and merciless creditor;—these are the dark shadows upon a great national character, and a national story of the deepest interest.

On the other hand, their history shows, as no other can, the folly and wickedness of that most deadly, though sometimes most fair-seeming, of all Satanic influences, religious persecution. Our fathers were wont in those evil times to enlarge with horror on the sin of the Jew in obstinately rejecting

Christ. In the day when account will be required of all, may it not be found that the deadliest of their own sins was, that by their hideous travesty of the Christian faith they shut out from the Jew the knowledge of the reality?

For centuries the bitterest persecutions came from those who, while robbing and ill-treating the Jews, because they charged them with heaping ridicule upon Christianity and eagerly aiding its enemies, were themselves ignorant of the first principles of the Gospel, and devoted adherents of the Church of those times. As the Reformation of the Church developed, and as the power of evangelical principles has increased, the persecution of the Jew has ceased. More and more has the Church everywhere realized the truth, that Christ died for the Jew no less than for the Gentile, and that He can be better served in this respect by the proclamation of His own loving message of forgiveness, than by any attempts to usurp His function as Judge, or to compel an outward submission, in which the heart has no part.

Israel has, indeed, a heavy account against the Anglo-Saxon race, though, it may be, not so heavy as against the Goth, the Teuton, and the Slav. There is some comfort in reflecting that we in this century have done somewhat to reduce the balance that stands against us. May our children learn the lesson of mercy and toleration in all its fulness, and so make such reparation as is possible for the mistakes and sins of our fathers!

FOOTNOTES:

[1] A Jew would doubtless deny this. I do not pursue the question further, as this is not a work of controversial theology; and, besides, the point has been made so clear by Christian divines that there can be no need of any advocacy of mine. Let the reader who may have any doubt on the subject consider Isa. xl. 10; xlv. 24; xlviii. 17; Jer. xxiii. 6; Hosea i. 7; Zech. ii. 10, 11; Malachi iii. 1, where not the title Elohim only, but that of Jehovah, is given to the Messiah.

[2] No question has been more disputed than whether the Sanhedrim, during the rule of the Roman Procurators, possessed the power of putting to death persons convicted of capital crimes. The statement made, St. John xviii. 31, and the action of Albinus, who, a.d. 63, deposed the High Priest Ananus, because the Sanhedrim had put St. James to death without his sanction, seem conclusive that they could not capitally punish persons *convicted of blasphemy*, unless under the Procurator's order. The case of St. Stephen, Acts viii., does not disprove this; for that was evidently a tumultuary

procedure, no sentence having been pronounced. But the Sanhedrim certainly had the power of capitally punishing *some* offenders, as, for instance, any Gentile passing beyond the barrier between the Temple Courts (see Jos. *B.J.* vi. 2, 4), an offence closely resembling blasphemy. Possibly they could inflict death for certain specified crimes, but only for these. It would be quite consistent with the principle of Roman government to allow the High Priests to punish capitally persons convicted of grave moral offences, but not such as were only guilty in matters relating 'to their own superstitions,' as they would phrase it.

[3] Acts iii. 17.

[4] St. Luke xxiii. 34.

[5] See Appendix I.

[6] 'Ye shall not see Me, until the time come when ye shall say, Blessed is He that cometh in the name of the Lord' (St. Luke xiii. 35)—that is, 'ye shall not apprehend Me, and the blessings I come to bring you, until you acknowledge Me as the true Messiah and Saviour of the world.' To '*see*' the Lord is, in the New Testament phrase, spiritually to discern and understand Him.

[7] *Betrothed*, chap. 31.

PART II
FROM THE BEGINNING OF THE FOURTEENTH CENTURY TO THE PRESENT TIME

CHAPTER XXI
A.D. 1300-1400. THE JEWS IN FRANCE

The history of the Jews in France, in the thirteenth century, may be regarded as terminating with their second expulsion from that country by Philip the Fair. That king died in 1314, and was succeeded by Louis X., called in history Hutin, or Mutin (the Turbulent). One of the first acts of the new king was to recall the Jews, who not only consented to return to a land where for generations past they had experienced nothing but harsh and contemptuous usage, but even to pay a heavy price for the privilege. Nothing gives us a stronger idea of the utter helplessness and friendlessness of the Hebrew people at this period than the readiness with which they would accept any conditions whatever that seemed to promise them protection for the moment against violent or lawless outrage. A semblance of justice, indeed, was shown them: their synagogues were restored to them, and their worship again permitted; they recovered the privilege of burying their dead in their ancient graveyards. Nay, such debts as were still owing to them—the greater portion having been already paid over to the king, who had condescended to make himself their trustee—they were allowed to claim before the public tribunals, conditionally always on their paying two-thirds of it into the royal treasury.[131] In the reign of Philip the Long, a few years afterwards, something like fairness and even mercy seems to have been shown them, possibly as a set-off to the king's exaction of 150,000 livres from them. They were allowed to lend on usury to certain persons and on certain conditions; they might acquire property in houses and land; and they were not required to wear their distinguishing badge while travelling from one town to another.

About this time (a.d. 1319) a novel charge was preferred against them, and which we might believe to have been at least founded on fact, if it did not seem impossible that the Jews of those times could have been guilty of such suicidal rashness. At Lunel they were accused of travestying the Saviour's passion—not (as was the ordinary charge) by the crucifixion of a Christian boy—but by carrying a crucifix in a public procession, reviling it as they went, dragging it through mire and filth, and heaping reproaches upon it.[132] For this offence they were tried, convicted, and punished.

But in 1321 a far more serious calamity befell them. It has been recorded that during the captivity in the East of Louis IX. a multitude of peasants assembled, and declared themselves commissioned from on high to rescue their beloved sovereign from bondage, and they had evidenced their zeal in the cause of Heaven by acts of barbarity towards the Jews. There was no king to be rescued now; but the Holy Land itself was in bondage, and there were vague prophecies current among them that it could be reconquered only by the mean and lowly. They were headed by a degraded priest and mendicant friar, who affected special sanctity of life, and claimed to work miracles in proof of their sacred mission. They were followed by large multitudes, who ravaged the southern provinces of France, and especially Languedoc, everywhere breaking open the prisons, and swelling their ranks by enlisting the criminals whom they let loose. They spared their Christian fellow-subjects as much as they could, but displayed the most relentless barbarity towards the Jews, whom they everywhere pillaged, outraged, and murdered. The Jews appealed to the Pope and to the king. The former issued an anathema against the insurgents, but it was altogether disregarded; the latter sent a few horsemen to their aid, who, however, were utterly powerless to help them. They fled in despair to the shelter of any fortified places which would refuse admittance to the Shepherds. Five hundred found a refuge in a castle at Verdun, on the Garonne, which the governor allowed them to occupy. Their enemies followed and besieged them. After a stout and desperate defence, finding themselves unable to hold out any longer, they threw some of their children over the walls, and then (as at Masada and at York) slew each other to a man. When the besiegers broke in, they found no living enemy!

All over Languedoc, at Angouleme, and at Bordeaux, frightful massacres of Jews took place. The excuse alleged for them was, that the plunder of the Jews was necessary to the 'armies of the Lord,' in order to equip them properly for the recovery of Palestine. But, terrible as were their sufferings from the violence of the fanatics, what ensued was even more full of horror. The outbreak was followed, as might have been anticipated, by an epidemic pestilence—the natural result of the scarcity of wholesome food and the corruption of so many human carcases. But the people, possessed as they were by the worst form of religious mania, were easily persuaded by their leaders that the malady was caused by the poisoning of wells and rivers, which again was the work of the Jews. The Sieur de Parthenay wrote word to the king that 'a great leper, seized on his land, had confessed to him that he had received from a rich Jew a consignment of drugs, which were to be enclosed in bags and thrown into the wells.'[133] The king returned in alarm from Poitou, which he had been visiting, and ordered that all lepers should be arrested and put to the question—that is, examined by torture. This mode of inquiry elicited the usual results. The unhappy sufferers in their agony confessed everything of which they had been suspected, however monstrous or incredible it might be. It appeared that there had been a conspiracy between the infidel kings of Tunis and Granada, the Jews, and the lepers, Satan himself presiding at the conference. Woe and misery were to be wrought on the Christians by the poisoning of the water which they drank. The lepers were straightway ordered to be burned, pregnant women alone being spared, and they only until the time of their delivery. In the instance of the Jews not even this mercy seems to have been shown: they were burned without distinction. At Chignon a great trench was dug, fires were kindled in it, and 160 Jews burned alive—men and women together. Many women, with their children in their arms, voluntarily threw themselves into the flames to escape baptism. In the royal prison at Vitry forty Jews, who were persuaded that no mercy would be shown them, resolved to die by their own hands rather than by those of the uncircumcised. They therefore fixed upon one of their own number, an aged man greatly honoured and beloved, and requested him to become their executioner. He consented to undertake the office, with the help of a youth whom he chose for the purpose. When all but these two had been slain, the old man ordered the youth to kill him also. He was obeyed; but the young man, lacking the resolution to take his own life, attempted to escape from the prison, when he was taken prisoner, and confessed what had taken place.

In the midst of these horrors Philip V. died (a.d. 1322), and his successor, Charles IV., was pleased to pardon the hapless survivors of this bloody persecution—conditionally, however, on the payment of a large subsidy. When this had been received, the Jews were permitted to leave their prisons, gather together what they could of their effects, and leave the kingdom. It is evident, however, that the whole Hebrew population could not have quitted the country; or, if they did, they soon began to return unnoticed to it, for in 1348, when a second visitation of the same terrible disease once more desolated the land, we find that the old calumny was renewed, and with the same merciless result, the sword of the law being let loose to slay those whom the pestilence had spared. Indeed, it is evident that, notwithstanding their multiplied miseries and wrongs, the Jews were still anxious to obtain the permission of their persecutors to reside among them, for we find them in 1360 bargaining with King John (who had been defeated and captured by the Black Prince) to supply him with the means of paying the ransom due from him, conditionally on their being permitted to dwell in France without molestation for the space of twenty years. A Jew named Manasseh (or Menecier, as he was styled) conducted the bargain on the part of the Jews. The fee for readmission to France was fixed at fourteen florins for each adult; for children and servants, one florin. Similarly, the annual fee for continued residence was seven florins and one florin. They were to be exempted from all taxes except land-tax. They were to be allowed to hold landed property, build synagogues, and possess cemeteries, and to be exempted from baronial jurisdiction, being placed directly under that of the king himself. They were also exempted from what had been always felt by them a heavy burden—the necessity of listening to controversial sermons, preached in the hope of converting them.

It was not without difficulty that the regent, afterwards Charles V., called the Wise, enforced the observance of these conditions, as he seems to have done in all good faith. Not long after his accession the clergy in Languedoc published a sentence of excommunication against all who should supply the Jews with fire or water, bread or wine. But, on receiving an appeal against this severity, the king issued his ordinance annulling the decree, as being alike unjust to the Jews and dishonourable to the Church. He twice renewed the compact with the Jews, once for six and once for ten years, receiving for the renewal 3000 gold livres. It is evident that during this interval of repose the wealth of the detested race had again accumulated. In 1378 they lent Charles 20,000 livres, and engaged to provide him with 200 more every week. But the usual result followed: the people began to clamour at the heavy burdens laid upon them, which they declared were imposed only for the purpose of ministering to the greed and luxury of the usurers. In the September of 1380 Charles V. died, and was succeeded by his son, a minor twelve years old. Soon after, a tumultuous outbreak took place in consequence of the regent, the Duke of Anjou, having confirmed the privilege granted to the Jews by the late king. All classes joined in it. The nobles, who, as usual, were deeply indebted to the Hebrew usurers, called out for their expulsion from the country, as the readiest mode of clearing themselves of their liabilities; the people, instigated probably by them, pillaged and destroyed the offices where the registers of debts were kept, and further gratified their enmity to the hateful race by plundering their houses of such valuables as they could lay their hands on, and by tearing their children from them and carrying them to the churches, where the clergy were always ready to baptize them. The regent endeavoured to suppress the disturbance; he issued a proclamation requiring all persons, on pain of death, to restore the spoil of which they had possessed themselves. But we are told that very few obeyed the order.

The regent persisted, however, in the policy he had adopted; and during the earlier years of Charles VI.'s reign the Jews were treated by the State with equity and mercy. But the evil lay too deep for any legislation to remedy. The distress of the country increased, and with it the difficulty of obtaining money. There was but one class from which money could be obtained, the Jews—and they unwisely abused the power thus put into their hands. Regardless of the angry passions which they were rousing, they continued their ruinous rates of usury until about fourteen years after the accession of Charles VI. Then the storm burst suddenly upon them, and they were once more commanded to quit the country. The step in question was taken in consequence of the condition into which the unfortunate young monarch had now sunk. His melancholy madness rendered him peculiarly liable to the influence of the clergy, who were for ever representing to him the guilt of standing between an accursed people and the vengeance of the God whom they had offended. The queen was won over to side with the persecuting party. The clergy, the nobles, and the people already belonged to it. Nothing for a long time had stood between the Jews and the sentence of banishment but the justice of the king. This barrier was now removed, and the blow fell heavily and suddenly. They were suffered to depart on milder terms than on previous occasions. Leave was given them to recover all debts due to them, and to sell their property as advantageously as they could. But they were allowed only one month in which to wind up their affairs, and then they crossed for the last time the frontiers of France.[134]

FOOTNOTES:

[131] It is noteworthy that this very scant and dubious measure of justice is acknowledged by Rabbi Joshua in terms of great thankfulness. 'He allowed the Jews,' says Joshua, 'to live in his kingdom, for they found favour in his eyes; and he accepted their persons.'

[132] It may be doubted whether this was not a simple attempt to celebrate the Feast of Purim—*the* feast in which

they took such special delight. Possibly the supposed crucifix was the figure of Haman on his gallows. See Appendix V.

[133] The supposed composition of the drugs in question shows an amount of ignorance, grossness of thought, and irreverence, which it would be difficult to match in all history: 'Fiebant de sanguine humano et urinâ cum tribus herbis. Ponebatur etiam Corpus Christi, et cum essent omnia desiccata usque ad pulverem terebantur.'

[134] No formal decree for their restoration was subsequently made, but it is at least doubtful whether the exclusion was rigidly enforced, even in the ages immediately following the decree of banishment. In some places—as for instance Metz—they do not seem to have been meddled with.

CHAPTER XXII
A.D. 1300-1400. THE JEWS IN ITALY

The attentive reader cannot fail to have noticed how scant has been the mention in these pages of the condition of the Jews in Italy. Little has been recorded of them, except that under the rule of the Lombard kings they were uniformly treated with humanity and justice, and that some few of the popes had issued decrees, advising what in these times we should regard as stern measures to be adopted for their conversion, while others forbade any such severities to be employed. But the silence of history respecting them is in itself significant, showing that no social convulsions disturbed the order of their daily lives, no flagrant wrongs and cruelties called out for mention. This is, at first sight at least, surprising. Considering that the clergy throughout what are called the Middle Ages were the persistent adversaries of the Jews, and that Italy was the very centre and source whence the clergy derived their inspiration, we should certainly have expected that the Jews of that country would experience the very extremity of intolerance and harshness. The fact that they received milder treatment than their neighbours is due to a variety of causes, which may be briefly touched on.

In the first place, the condition of Italy was different, during those ages, from that of other European countries. The feudal system, the source, as we have seen, of so many of the wrongs and miseries of the Jews, was never so firmly established there as in the other European countries, and it died out much earlier. The great free cities exercised an authority of their own, independent of any feudal superior, and in these the rights of the Jews were maintained almost as inflexibly as those of the Christians. The continued strife between Pope and Emperor, Guelf and Ghibelline, so largely engaged the attention of the Italian nation as to allow them little leisure to trouble themselves with the affairs of a people who were contented to live in peace, and whose aid was often found extremely serviceable by the dominant party. It is certain again, whatever may have been the reason, that the fanatical spirit which was so easily roused, and in such fatal excess, in France and Germany, languished and soon died out on the Italian side of the Alps. The cry that the Holy Sepulchre had again fallen into the possession of the infidels found but a feeble echo in the streets of Naples,[135] Rome, and

Florence; nor do the people seem to have argued, as they did throughout France and Germany, and even occasionally in Spain, that the outrages charged upon the Mahometans of Palestine were to be expiated by the Jews of Europe.

Again, as a rule, though doubtless with many exceptions, the popes were more merciful to them than were the sovereigns of any other Christian land. Some pontiffs, as, for example, Gregory I., Innocents II. and IV., Alexander IV., Nicolases III. and V., Martin V., and others, showed them marked favour; while others, if they evinced no partiality, at least discouraged persecution, disregarded idle charges, and would allow no violence. Some doubtless issued harsh decrees and curtailed the privileges granted by their predecessors, but such oppression as John of England, Philip Augustus, and Philip the Fair of France exhibited in their dealings with their Hebrew subjects may fairly be said to have been unknown among them. This was in most instances due to the fact that the popes, however low may have been the moral standard of many among them, were as a rule men of cultivation and intelligence, in whose ears the popular charges against the Jews must needs have sounded as idle calumnies.[136] Many among them also were wise enough—if it was only worldly wisdom—to know that conversions effected by force were many degrees worse than unconverted obstinacy, and on that ground forbade such to be attempted.[137]

But there was another and a weightier reason for the immunity from persecution enjoyed by the Jews; and that was, that they were not the sole—in truth, not even the chief—usurers and money-lenders in Italy. The Caorsini, as the Italian bankers were called (presumably from their having first practised their calling in Cahors), were the persons employed by the popes to collect their revenues, an office almost everywhere else entrusted to the Jews. The Caorsini carried on business, though only to a trifling extent, comparatively speaking, in other lands, notably France and England. Henry III. would have expelled them from England if they had not claimed the protection of the Holy Father. It is probably to them that Bernard of Clairvaulx refers when he speaks of usurers more exorbitant in their demands than the Jews themselves. If indeed it is true that their practice was to demand five per cent. per month (after the first month[138]) for their loans, this charge is justifiable enough. These Italian usurers drove a trade in their native land, which, if it did not monopolize the business of the country, at all events threw all competition into the shade. They farmed the tribute and taxes of all kinds levied by the popes on the Christian kingdoms of Europe. They provided subsidies for crowned heads, advanced sums on mortgage to the nobles, and loans to merchants and small traders, and were popularly said to be worse Jews than the Hebrews themselves.

There were doubtless many Jewish merchants—and wealthy ones—in the great Italian cities, who carried on an extensive and profitable business in money-lending. But they were not, as in neighbouring lands, the universal creditors, and therefore escaped the general detestation entertained for their brethren elsewhere.

Indeed, the mere fact that the grandson of Peter Leonis, a converted Jew, was not only allowed to mix in familiar intercourse with the noblest families in Rome, but was actually raised to the papal chair (a.d. 1130), under the title of Anacletus II., sufficiently shows in how widely different a light the Jews were regarded in Italy and other European countries. No doubt his Hebrew origin was continually thrown in his teeth by his adversaries. But his election to the pontificate is a fact beyond dispute.[139]

We may note also the different course pursued in Naples (a.d. 1260) by the Italian rulers from that ordinarily adopted on such occasions in other countries. At Trani, in the Neapolitan territory, the Jews had been protected and favoured by Frederick II., to whom they had rendered many signal services. On his death-bed he commended them to the protection of the States, who, however, adopted the opinion, common enough in those times, that the greatest service they could do the Jews was by obliging them to turn Christians. To avoid the persecution which was imminent, they agreed to change their faith, conditionally on being allowed to intermarry with the noblest families in the kingdom. A good deal of indignation was excited by this permission, and this rose to a greater height when several relapses took place. To punish them a monk at Trani buried a cross in a dunghill, and then accused a Jew belonging to the city of the sacrilege. A riot was the result, in which not only the supposed criminal, but all his countrymen in the town, were murdered. The outbreak extended to Naples, and similar scenes of bloodshed would have ensued, if the authorities had not intervened. Alexander IV., the reigning pope, issued a proclamation requiring the rioters to desist; the king and the nobles lent their authority, and the *émeute* was suppressed before much blood had been shed.

In the fourteenth century, which we have now more especially under consideration, the first thing we have to note is, the proposal of Pope Clement V., who in 1308, three years after his accession to office, removed the seat of papal government to Avignon, where the popes continued to exercise undisputed authority for a period of seventy years. Clement V. is a ruler for whom little admiration or respect can be obtained. Nevertheless, his suggestion—if it did not amount to an order—that a Hebrew professorship should be established in every European university, in order that the Church might gain a complete knowledge of the Hebrew language and literature, and so be enabled the more effectually to promote the conversion of the

Jews, deserves our notice and respect. The words may have proceeded out of the mouth of iniquity and falsehood, but they are nevertheless the words of righteousness and truth.

Clement's successor, John XXII. (a.d. 1316), adopted a different policy towards the Jews, having been incited to it, it is said, by his sister, who accused them of having insulted a cross which was being carried in a procession in which she herself, in company with some bishops, was taking part. He straightway published an edict banishing all Jews from the territories of the Church; but the edict was revoked soon afterwards, Robert of Jerusalem having interceded in their behalf, and a bribe of one hundred thousand florins paid to the pope's sister.

Clement VI. (a.d. 1342) bears a character in history for luxury and dissipation which is hardly surpassed by the vilest of the occupants of the papal chair; but his single good point—kindness of heart—was exhibited in his endeavours to suppress the persecution of the Jews, and the friendly shelter which he afforded to such of the unhappy race as sought refuge in his dominions.

The absence from Rome of the popes during the seventy years which elapsed between the settlement of Clement V. at Avignon, and the appointment, in 1378, of an antipope in the person of Urban VI., renders the history of the Jews during this century unusually meagre. But they appear to have lived unmolested in the various Italian towns. They must have been on good terms with the pope's legate at Bologna, where they presented him with a copy of the Old Testament Scriptures, said to have been written by Ezra himself. This is still preserved, we are told, in the library of the Dominicans in that city. They were protected also by the Venetian government, which allowed them to settle as bankers in their city. They were careful, however, to maintain a strict supervision over them, and in 1385 obliged them to live within the Ghetto, as the Jewish quarter in an Italian city is usually styled.

Learning flourished in Italy among the Jews during this century. The recently founded universities were thronged with Jewish students, and classical literature was especially studied. There were several scholars among them of great repute. Pre-eminently conspicuous are Immanuel ben Solomon and Moses Rieti. The former of these, regarded by the Jews as the greatest of their poets, and said to have been the friend of Dante, wrote a work on Paradise and Hell which is an imitation of the *Divina Commedia* of the great Italian. He wrote also religious poetry and several commentaries on the Old Testament Scriptures.

FOOTNOTES:

[135] In the Norman kingdom of Naples, where the feudal system had a firmer hold than in any other part of Italy, the Jews were more severely treated; but even there, as we shall see, persecution was promptly and firmly checked.

[136] The absurd charges alleged against the Jews were not confined to the crucifying of Christian boys, poisoning of rivers, and insults offered to the consecrated wafer. In Innocent III.'s pontificate they were accused of selling the milk of their women as common milk, in order that Christian children might be brought up on it, and so (it is presumed) imbibe Jewish opinions. It was said that they trampled the grapes in the winepresses in linen stockings, drawing out the best wine for themselves and leaving the refuse for the Christians, in the hope that they would use it in the administration of the Holy Eucharist!

[137] It is a curious fact that the Jews sometimes received the severest treatment from pontiffs whose characters stood high for both justice and mercy, and sometimes were equitably and leniently dealt with by those from whose general character nothing but intolerance and harshness might have been expected. Innocent III. (a.d. 1198) was one of the greatest and best of those who have filled the papal chair—wise and far-sighted, just and merciful. Yet his language respecting the Jews is in the highest degree harsh and intolerant. He repeats the familiar charge that they are guilty of the blood of the Redeemer, and as such are branded with the curse of Cain. He denounces their employment by the State, even as collectors of the taxes, and threatens the severest chastisement to those who show them any favour. On the other hand, Innocent IV. (a.d. 1243), who succeeded to the papacy some fifty years afterwards, an inflexible and haughty bigot, issued a bull in favour of the Jews which is a perfect marvel for its humanity and justice. He denounces the cruelty and lawless violence with which they were treated. He treats with merited scorn the monstrous charges of sacrificing Christian boys in order to use their blood in the Paschal rites, and forbids such charges to be received. Nay,

he adds that if the accuser cannot sustain his charge by the evidence of three Christians and three Jews, he must himself undergo the punishment due to a murderer. Sometimes the pontiff and his edicts accord. Martin V.'s acts (a.d. 1417) towards the Jews bear the stamp of his generous character. He orders that all synagogues shall be protected, the Jewish worship permitted, all privileges, customs, and institutions maintained, unless any of these should be found subversive of public morality, or insulting to the Catholic faith. No compulsion is to be used to bring any Jew to baptism. No one is to disturb them in the celebration of their festivals. He repeals the order issued by the Dominicans, requiring them to hear controversial sermons. He gives them full licence to trade. The nineteenth century, in the most enlightened countries, has done little more for them.

[138] They charged no interest for the first month, thinking in that way to escape the odium of usury.

[139] Bernard of Clairvaulx, a zealous partisan of the rival pope, Innocent V., dilates on the outrage offered to Christ through the occupation of the seat of St. Peter by 'Judaica Soboles.' — *Bern. Epist.* 134.

CHAPTER XXIII
A.D. 1300-1400. THE JEWS IN GERMANY, THE LOW COUNTRIES, ETC

The history of the Jews in Germany throughout the fourteenth century is one long series of wrongs and barbarities. Almost immediately after its commencement, the disturbances at Nuremberg, which had been suppressed by Duke Albert some ten or twelve years previously, broke out afresh. In the course of these the mob, seizing on Mordecai, a Rabbi of learning and high repute, publicly hanged him. In the next generation, a man named Armleder, a publican by trade, incited an outbreak among the peasants of Alsatia with such fatal effect that more than 1500 Jews were slaughtered. In Swabia also great numbers were murdered; while at Deckendorf we are informed that the whole of the Hebrew inhabitants of the town were massacred, and their property pillaged or destroyed. There appear to have been no special grounds for these enormities. The whole atmosphere was, as it were, charged with deadly vapours, and the slightest spark of discontent was enough to cause a disastrous explosion. The authorities in some cases sided with the rioters; in others they stood aloof, and allowed them to work their pleasure; while in some few they interfered to stay the mischief if they could, generally with but little success. Great injury was also done to the Jews all over Germany, by the censure passed on them by Pope Clement V. for their excessive usury. Numberless lawsuits, we are told, were in consequence instituted against them, in which their right to recover money lent on interest by them was challenged. A few years subsequently the whole of the Hebrew population of Hungary was expelled from the country by Louis I., who displayed his intemperate zeal, not by that act only, but by his attempts, in concert with Casimir of Poland, to force the profession of Christianity on the Lithuanians.

But all those troubles, trying as they must have proved to the unfortunate Jews, were as nothing when compared with the terrible afflictions which that people were called upon to endure, in consequence of the outbreak of the fearful pestilence known in history by the name of the 'Black Death.' This appeared in Germany 1348, and was so fatal that the country was almost depopulated by it. It was sudden and rapid in its effects. Tumours, mostly of a black colour, made their appearance in the groin and axilla, accompanied by spitting of blood. In three days, at longest, the crisis was reached, and few survived it. The science of the day could not explain its origin, any more than it could cure, or even palliate, its virulence. In the absence of any reasonable explanation of the causes of the outbreak, the terrified multitude caught at whatever was suggested to them. It was first attributed to the indignation of Heaven at the outrageous wickedness of the age; and large bodies of men banded themselves together to make atonement for this by fasting and penitential discipline. They formed into companies, men and women, of all ranks and ages, naked to the waist, and marked with a red cross; and in this state marched in procession through the chief cities, scourging themselves as they went, and calling on all to follow them.

But a new and much more welcome theory was presently started—that the pestilence which was slaying its thousands and tens of thousands was due to the Jews. It is said that the Flagellants first suggested this; but there is little reason for supposing so. The first idea in the minds of uneducated men, when attacked by some malady of which they have had no previous experience, is that they have been poisoned or bewitched; the next, to fasten upon the person by whom the drug has been administered or the spell wrought. Now, it was argued, if this wickedness had been devised by any one, it must have been by some inveterate enemy of Christian men; and who were such inveterate enemies of Christian men as the Jews? They, in truth, and they only, were capable of malice so subtle and deadly! Again, it was clear that these operations had been carried on in some wholesale manner. The criminals must have infected the air or poisoned the water. The idea, once conceived, spread like wild fire. No inquiry was made; no proofs were called for. What need of them? It was clear as the day that the Jews had poisoned the wells and fountains! The supposed murderers were everywhere pursued with the most merciless barbarity. Some were dragged before the tribunals, where a form of trial was gone through. Some were slaughtered by the mob without any investigation at all. It mattered little which course was pursued. The result was invariably the same.

The persecution seems to have commenced in the autumn of 1348, at Chillon, in Geneva, where criminal proceedings were taken against them, on the specific charge of having poisoned the wells. The same inquiries took place in other towns, as Berne and Freiburg. Some poison had been found in a well at Zoffingen—though by whom put in there was no evidence to determine. But the usual mode of eliciting evidence in those ages was resorted to, and with the customary result. Balavignus, a Jewish physician resident at Thonon, having been put on the rack, confessed that

Rabbi Jacob, of Toledo, had sent him, by a Jewish boy, some poison in the mummy of an egg. The poison consisted of a powder, sewn up in a thin leathern pouch, and it was accompanied by a letter commanding him, on penalty of excommunication, to throw the powder into the principal wells of Thonon, in order to destroy the people who lived there. In obedience to this injunction he had distributed the poison in various places, and more particularly had thrown it into a spring on the shore near Thonon. He swore by the Law and the five Books of Moses that this confession was true, and also implicated several other Jews as accomplices. Another Jew, of Neustadt, named Banditono, was similarly put to the torture, and confessed to having thrown a packet of poison, given him by one of his brethren, into a well at Carulet, and denounced other Jews, whom he named, as having done the same. Eight others underwent the same treatment, and made confessions, all nearly resembling the two above quoted, with the difference that some admitted that the whole Jewish people, except those under seven years of age, were privy to and participators in the plot. It is wonderful that they did not implicate the infants in arms!

The persecution soon spread to neighbouring lands. At Basle the populace obliged their magistrates to take an oath that they would burn all the Jews in the town, and forbid any of their countrymen to settle in their country for two hundred years to come. In compliance with the order, all the Jews in the place were shut up in a wooden building and burnt alive. At Bennefeld, in Alsace, a diet was held, at which a similar decree was made. At Spires the Jews, driven to despair, shut themselves up, together with their wives and children, in their houses, which they then set on fire, and all perished in the flames. In Mentz and Eslingen similar tragedies were enacted. In the first-named city, when the Flagellants made their entrance, the Jews began by repelling the violence offered them; but, perceiving the impossibility of making any effectual resistance, they too fired their dwellings and destroyed themselves and all belonging to them. In Eslingen it was the synagogue, with the entire Hebrew population of the place, that was consumed; and it is related that mothers were seen to fling their children into the burning pile, to prevent their undergoing compulsory baptism. At Strasburg two thousand Jews were burned on a scaffold erected in their own burial-ground. For months the same cruelties were perpetrated along the Rhine and the contiguous cities. The history of these times is one unvaried repetition of horrors, which it wearies the pen to describe and sickens the heart to peruse. Everywhere there are the same groundless and monstrous charges, the same blind and fanatic fury, the same merciless and exterminating hate. And, worst of all, these atrocities are committed in the name of Christ and His Gospel! If we could conceive that the gates of hell had been broken open, and its inmates had overrun the earth, the deeds we might have expected of them were just what the rabble of these German cities actually performed. They did not, however, wholly escape the consequences of their own lawless cruelty. In many places the Jews, before inflicting death upon themselves, turned their swords against their persecutors, and inflicted severe retribution on them; while in Frankfort their despairing rage caused the destruction of the town-hall and cathedral and a large portion of the city.

It would not be just to omit the fact that several among the European sovereigns condemned these proceedings, and did their best to check them. Clement VI., a self-indulgent and easy-tempered man, whose reign was a continued scene of slack and voluptuous living, was nevertheless roused by the enormities of the wrongs which he saw perpetrated on the helpless Jews, to exert himself to the best of his power in arresting the popular frenzy and punishing the offenders. Charles of Moravia, also, Duke Albert of Austria, and others, would fain have saved them if they could. But the fury of the people would not be restrained, and Albert was obliged to condemn five hundred of them to the flames. In Lithuania alone were they permitted any respite. Here they were protected by Casimir III., King of Poland, known in history as the Great. He confirmed the privileges granted them by his predecessor Boleslaus, and bestowed additional favours on them. It is popularly believed that he was induced to show them this consideration by his attachment to a beautiful Jewess named Estherka.[140] It is at least certain that throughout his reign the Jews in Poland escaped persecution, and large numbers of Jews migrated to that country.

The history of the Jews in the Netherlands during the fourteenth century very nearly resembles that of their German brethren. They had settled long before in the Low Countries, where the trade had fallen almost entirely into their hands. Their numbers were swelled by fugitives from England and France, from which countries, as we have seen, they had been forcibly expelled. They were treated sometimes kindly, sometimes harshly, according to the caprice of the rulers and the people. They were expelled from the duchy of Brabant in 1370, on account of a charge of sacrilege, which was very frequently made in mediæval times. It was said that they had stolen and then stabbed the holy wafer at Brussels, which bled profusely. A banker of Enghien, named Jonathan, was charged as the chief offender, on the evidence of a woman, who confessed to having been an accomplice. All the Jews suspected were put to torture, and afterwards torn with red-hot pincers, and then burned.[141]

Such Jews as had taken refuge in Bohemia do not appear to have fared much better than their brethren in other European countries. The

Emperor Wenceslaus, son of Charles IV., a lavish and dissipated sovereign, anxious to recover the goodwill of his subjects, whom he had alienated by his excesses, issued a decree discharging all his nobles from any liabilities they might have incurred to the Jews. The people thereupon, who had been afraid to meddle with them, because they regarded them as living under royal protection, considering that they had now lost the emperor's favour, broke out into a riot at Gotha, where they massacred large numbers of them. They were presently joined by the peasants, and the outbreak extended to other cities. At Spires the whole of the Jewish residents, with the exception of some few small children, who were reserved for the font, were put to the sword.

Soon afterwards the cry was raised again that the springs and rivers had been poisoned; and the Jews were subjected to a second persecution all over Germany, and in parts of Italy and France. We are informed that the emperor was fully convinced of the falsehood of the accusation—which, indeed, it is difficult to believe that any person of sense and education could ever have credited. But it was in vain to attempt to reason with the multitude; and, despairing of obtaining peace or quiet in his kingdom so long as the Jews were allowed to reside in it, he issued an order requiring them either to accept Christianity or depart from the empire. The observation, already made in the instance of other lands, naturally recurs to us when we read his sentence. What punishment could it be to them to leave a country where they had been so persistently and so remorselessly wronged? Nevertheless, it is evident that it *was* a punishment, and a severe one to them. It is to their honour that few of them accepted the alternative offered them, but went forth into exile, with all its sorrows and privations, rather than forsake their ancient faith.

The reader will not wonder that in an age of such unexampled misery, few German Jews were distinguished for their literary success. Isaac of Düren, Alexander Cohen of Cologne, Halevi of Mentz, Isserlein of Marburg, and Lipman of Mulhouse, were among the most celebrated writers of these unhappy times.

FOOTNOTES:

[140] *i.e.*, Little Esther. Some historians have doubted this story. They point out that Casimir's demeanour towards the Jews was only of a piece with his conduct towards the lower classes of his subjects generally. He showed so great a

regard for the rights of the despised serfs that he was called 'the Peasant King.' Again, it is certain that Casimir's edict is dated 1343, and his connection with Estherka did not begin till 1350. On the other hand, Casimir's one weakness was his passion for women, and the Polish historians say distinctly that Estherka gained great privileges from him for her people. Probably both explanations are correct. He granted the edict of 1343 from a sense of justice, and the monopolies of the Jews, later in his reign, at Estherka's entreaty.

[141] In 1820 a commemoration of this miracle took place in St. Gudule, when eighteen pictures were painted for the church, describing the entire action of the story, the tortures of the Jews being minutely depicted.

CHAPTER XXIV
A.D. 1300-1400. THE JEWS IN SPAIN

Up to this time, as has been already remarked, the Spanish Jews had enjoyed a freedom from persecution which presents a favourable contrast to the monstrous wrongs and cruelties which they underwent in other lands. The fourteenth century witnessed the gathering of the storm which, in that which ensued, was to burst with such deadly fury on the devoted race; nor were they even now exempt from occasional foretastes of its visitation. At its outset Ferdinand IV., known in Spanish history as 'the Summoned,'[142] a youth at that time under age, occupied the throne, but the administration of affairs was in the hands of his mother, the queen regent. It should be noted that, although the Jews still retained the rights and privileges accorded them by previous generations, they were fast becoming odious in the eyes of all classes. The *haute noblesse* were jealous of the court favour which the Jews had so long enjoyed, and were seeking for an opportunity to oust them from it; the lesser nobles were deeply in their debt, and looked to a popular outbreak as the readiest mode of ridding themselves of their encumbrances; the priesthood were, as a rule, though with some noble exceptions, their bitter enemies, continually denouncing them to the people, as the causes of every national misfortune that befell them. This was partly due to religious bigotry, partly to their jealousy of the greater wealth and the superior medical skill of the Jews, which prevented them from acquiring the money and the influence over the people which a successful exercise of that profession would have ensured. As for the people, they were largely under the influence of the clergy, and readily believed the stories poured into their ears. Besides, the spectacle of the riches and luxury in which the Jews lived provoked at once their indignation and their rapacity. The train had been laid, and it needed nothing but the application of the spark to fire it.

Ferdinand's favourite minister was a Jew named Samuel, a man of great ability, and, it is said, of a haughty, imperious temper. His death was mysterious. An assassin, who was never discovered, entered his house, a.d. 1305, at Seville, and stabbed him to the heart. It was not difficult to guess at the motives or the instigators of the deed; but nothing was brought to light. His successor seems also to have been a Jew, for a league was formed among the grandees against him. They presented a petition to the Cortes, assembled at Medina del Campo, requesting that measures might be taken to restrain the insolence of the Jews. An order was passed, accordingly, that they should not in future be collectors of taxes.

This was soon followed up by other like attacks. In 1313, Rodrigo, Bishop of St. Jago, held a provincial council at Zamora, at which manifestoes were presented, which showed but too plainly how fast the animosity against the Jews was ripening. Several of the constitutions of the council breathe the same spirit. It was enacted that Jews, henceforth, shall hold no post or dignity; and any Jews who hold them shall resign such within thirty days. They shall not be admitted as witnesses against Christians, nor claim, as hitherto, the benefit of the laws. No Christian women shall be nurses to Jewish children. Jews shall not attend Christians as physicians. They are prohibited from inviting Christians to their feasts. They shall not associate with Christians, lest they teach them their errors.

Some of these decrees were re-enacted at the Councils of Burgos and Salamanca, in 1315 and 1322, where it was also ordered that any Christians should be excommunicated who were present at Jewish marriages; and any Jews who called themselves by Christian names should be punishable as heretics!

In 1325, Alphonso XI., son of Ferdinand IV., was declared to be of age. His first acts showed that, whatever might be the sentiments of the nobles, the clergy, or the people, he was resolved to uphold the Jews. He chose as his minister of finance, Joseph of Ecija, a Jew of great administrative ability; and one of his first acts was to declare null and void various bulls and prelates' letters, which had been obtained by persons owing debts to Jews, by which those debts were cancelled. He also granted the Jews licence to acquire landed property, though he limited the amount which they might hold. But he could not overcome the popular animosity against them. Don Joseph was presently accused of having, in concert with Count Alvar Osorio, bewitched the king by giving him magical potions. Osorio was sacrificed to these machinations; and Don Joseph, though he escaped on that occasion, was not long afterwards charged with keeping fraudulent accounts, and dismissed from his office. Probably, however, the king deprived him of his situation as the only mode of saving him from the malice of his enemies, for we find that he did not withdraw his friendship from him.[143]

In 1348, the king was induced to sign an order for the banishment of all Jews from his dominions, on account of an insult which they had offered to the Host, as it was being carried in procession through the streets. The order was cancelled, however, on the discovery being made that the supposed insult was a mere accident, and the person by whom it was thought to have been offered was a Christian. The revocation provoked a riot, which was with difficulty put down by a determined exercise of the royal authority.

This disturbance had hardly been quelled, when one more furious still broke out, caused by the spread of the plague, which had originated in Germany, into the Spanish peninsula. The cry was raised here, too, that the Jews had poisoned the waters of the Tagus—a crime impossible of commission! Nevertheless, on that indictment massacres were perpetrated in several of the cities, especially in Toledo, and 15,000 Jews are said to have been murdered.

During the reign of Pedro, called the Cruel, who succeeded in a.d. 1350, the Jews recovered all, and more than all, their former ascendency. Notwithstanding the prohibition of the law, Samuel Levi, a Jew, became the royal treasurer. He it was who built the famous synagogue at Toledo, which in its own peculiar style has no rival. He was a man of rare ability, and his administrative genius soon filled King Pedro's coffers; but, unhappily for himself, it filled his own also. A charge was brought against him of mal-administration of the revenues; and, though it does not appear that this was proved, it brought to light another and far more grievous offence—that of being too wealthy. He was sent to prison where he was racked, to oblige him to disclose the full extent of his riches, and he expired under the torture.

But though the king sacrificed his favourite minister to his own avarice, he did not withdraw his countenance from the Jews. They continued, to all outward appearance, to prosper; but the public hatred of them was ever on the increase, and the time approaching nearer and nearer when a heavy reckoning would have to be paid. Lopes de Ayala, the chancellor of the Count of Trastamara, afterwards king, under the title of Henry II., expresses the general sentiment of the Spanish people respecting them. He describes them as 'the blood-suckers of the afflicted people, as men who exact fifty per cent., eighty, a hundred—.... Through them,' he writes, 'the land is desolate; ... tears and groans affect not their hard hearts; their ears are deaf to petitions for delay.' Much of Pedro's unpopularity was due to the favour he showed to this people. He was himself stigmatized as a Jew. It was affirmed that he was the child of a Hebrew mother, who had been substituted for the true Infant of Spain. The Jews stood bravely by him, and suffered heavily in consequence. Many were slain for espousing his cause at Toledo, many more at Nejara; and at Monteil, where the final struggle between Pedro and Henry took place, the slaughter of Jews was enormous.

But Henry, when once seated on the throne (a.d. 1369), was too politic a ruler to alienate such useful servants of the crown as the Jews had proved themselves to be. He pursued the traditionary policy towards them, interposing the shield of his protection between them and the hostile people. To the remonstrances addressed to him by the Cortes against their occupation of posts of dignity and importance, or possessing the same rights and advantages enjoyed by Christians, he simply replied that he considered it right that their ancient status should continue.

Henry died a.d. 1379, and was succeeded by John I., who pursued the policy of his father and grandfather, so far as the Jews were concerned, refusing to listen to the angry remonstrances continually addressed to him by the Cortes respecting them. Early in his reign occurred the strange but successful plot of the Jews against their countryman, Joseph Pichon, a man of wealth and influence, holding the office of Crown Treasurer. They had apparently become jealous of his favour with the king, and resolved on compassing his death. They applied accordingly to John for a warrant to punish a convicted unbeliever,[144] though without revealing his name. The king having unsuspiciously signed it, they bribed the executioner to put the sentence immediately into effect, and Pichon was seized and beheaded, without having even been informed for what crime he was arraigned. The king, when he discovered the trick that had been played on him, was extremely indignant. He punished the immediate authors of the crime with death, and deprived the Jews of the right of determining their own causes.

The king's influence was to some extent successful in restraining the popular hatred of the Jews. But when he died, a.d. 1390, and was succeeded by his son, Henry III., a lad eleven years old, there was another popular outbreak. Ferdinand Martinez, Archdeacon of Ecija, had, during the reign of John, been continually in the habit of reviling the Jews, and stirring up the populace to attack them. The late king had discountenanced his proceedings; but he was no sooner removed than Martinez threw aside all restraint, and by his harangues roused the smouldering hatred towards the Jews, which had long possessed the people, into a fierce and destructive flame. The Jews' quarter was attacked. Pillage, murder, violation, followed; four thousand were slaughtered, the archdeacon heading the mob, and urging them on to still greater atrocities. No steps were taken to punish the perpetrators of this violence. The contagion soon spread to other cities. In Cordova, in Valencia, in Burgos, in Toledo, in Barcelona, in Pampeluna, and other towns of Aragon and Navarre, there were similar massacres. As many as two hundred thousand Jews are said to have been forced to receive baptism. Such as escaped with their lives were stripped of all their possessions, and their houses plundered and burned.

King Henry III., who, like many other sovereigns, was largely dependent on the Jews for the maintenance of his revenues, was reduced to great straits to support his household expenses. An anecdote is related of him which, if true, curiously illustrates the history of those times. He is said to have found his exchequer so low one day as to be obliged to pawn his cloak to pay for his supper. He was informed that in the palace of the archbishop an entertainment was in progress, at which every delicacy was provided in profuse abundance. He repaired thither in disguise, and learned not only that the wealth of the revellers had been truly reported, but that it had been amassed by fraud and peculation. The next day he sent for the grandees of the court, and among them the archbishop, and inquired of him, 'How many kings have you known in Spain?' The archbishop answered, 'Three—your grandfather, your father, and yourself.' 'Nay,' rejoined Henry; 'young as I am, I can remember at least twenty, though there ought to have been only one. But it is time that I put my rivals down, and reign alone.' At the same moment a band of soldiers, accompanied by an executioner, and carrying ropes and gibbets, entered the apartment. The grandees threw themselves at his feet, and entreated his mercy. He spared their lives, but required a strict account of their management of his affairs, obliging them to refund large sums which they had embezzled.

Many Spanish Jews were eminent in literature during this century. Rabbi Abner, the physician, known as a Jewish writer previously to his conversion, wrote afterwards an able refutation of Kimchi's work against Christianity. Solomon Levi, also a convert to the Gospel, is known in history as the Bishop of Burgos, a learned and successful writer. This also is the age of Don Santo de Cañon, the celebrated troubadour, who, like the two before mentioned, renounced Judaism for Christianity.

FOOTNOTES:

[142] Ferdinand had condemned to death two cavaliers named Carvajal, on a charge of murder, refusing to hear their defence. Immediately before their execution they summoned Ferdinand to answer for his unjust sentence before the tribunal of God within a month. He died exactly a month afterwards.

[143] A strange, almost incredible story is told of the fate of Joseph. Gonzales, master of Calatrava, offered to pay 800 lbs. of silver into the king's treasury, conditionally on his making over to him eight of the principal Jews of the

kingdom, to be dealt with as he pleased. The king consented. Gonzales seized Joseph, and Samuel, the king's physician, and put them to the torture, to compel them to surrender the whole of their wealth. They died under the infliction; but he obtained enormous sums from them and his other prisoners. Gonzales was raised to great honour, and made Bishop of Alcantara. He afterwards forfeited the king's favour, was arrested as a traitor, and beheaded.

[144] The probable explanation is, that they knew Pichon was meditating a change of religion, the scandal of which they were anxious to prevent.

CHAPTER XXV
A.D. 1400-1500. THE JEWS IN GERMANY AND ITALY

The records of the Jews in Central Europe during this century are unusually scanty. They had been—nominally, at all events—expelled from various parts of it; and, though it is very probable that they were permitted, through contempt or compassion, to linger on in their old homes, yet they would be careful, as far as possible, to avoid notice. In Poland alone they seem to have flourished in prosperity and peace, and to have received large accessions of members from less kindly disposed countries.

But we hear something, nevertheless, of them. In Guelderland they were numerous, and lived securely under the protection of its rulers, particularly in the cities of Zutphen, Doesborg, and Arnheim. In the last-named city a Jew was even appointed the physician to the town; and decrees were issued prohibiting, on severe penalties, any ill-treatment of Jews in public or private. On the other hand, a singular fact occurred during this century, which seems to manifest the very opposite state of feeling. A noble lady of Guelderland having married a Jew, was regarded as an adulteress for having so done, and was burnt alive at Cologne for the offence. The Jews also were driven out of the neighbouring city of Utrecht in 1444; nor were they allowed to return to Holland until after the revolution of 1795. Commercial jealousy was probably the cause of this expulsion.

In 1453 there were Jewish riots in various parts of Silesia, and particularly in Breslau, where more than forty Jews were burnt. In the following year Ladislaus, King of Hungary, allowed his subjects to drive the Jews out of his dominions, seize on their houses and lands, and cancel all debts due to them. The only conditions he required of them, in return for this permission, was their making good to him the tribute which had been paid by the Jews. These outbreaks appear to have been caused (as was so frequently the case, both in previous and subsequent generations) by the influence of fanatical monks, who made the tour of Central Europe, denouncing the Jews as the enemies of God and man, and calling on all Christian men to avert the displeasure of Heaven by slaying and expelling them. A preacher named Capistran in this manner raised commotions in Silesia, and in Southern Germany Bernard produced the same disastrous effects. In Styria, late in the century, the people petitioned Maximilian to be permitted to drive the Jews out, as their Hungarian neighbours had done in the previous generation. They alleged the old charge of kidnapping and murdering children, and offered him 30,000 florins as a compensation for the loss of the Jewish tribute. We read that they were expelled accordingly in 1496. Similar expulsions took place in Mentz, Nuremberg, and Trent. In the latter place the accidental death of a child—attributed, as usual, to the Jews—was the cause of their banishment. But the mania for the removal of the Jews from all the countries of Europe—either because their presence was held to be like that of leeches fastening on the human frame and draining its life-blood, or because it was feared that the vengeance of Heaven would visit all those who offered shelter or kindness to its enemies—seems now to have taken the place of the thirst for their blood which distinguished the ages immediately preceding. The idea was quite as unreasonable and unjust, but a shade less horrible and revolting.

In Italy, as in previous generations, the Jews, if they did not receive the full rights of humanity, were at least treated with toleration, and even some degree of kindness. The demeanour of the popes towards them was, as before, very capricious—varying, in fact, with the religious convictions or state policy of each succeeding pontiff. In 1417, when the schism of the double papacy came to an end through the unanimous election of Martin V., the Jews marched, according to ancient custom, in the papal procession, with lighted torches, chanting Hebrew Psalms, and presenting to the newly-made Pope a copy of the Pentateuch. Martin V. received it with a benediction, and a prayer that the veil might be removed from their eyes, so that they might rightly understand the Law. He then issued a proclamation, in which they were dealt with mercifully and justly. Their synagogues, their form of worship, their privileges, usages, and institutions were to be respected, so only that they offered no affront to the Christian faith. No forcible attempts were to be made to baptize their children, and no one was to interrupt their festivals. With Pope Eugenius IV., who succeeded in 1431, the condition of things was changed. The stern and inflexible character, so forcibly exhibited in his dealings with the Council of Basle and the Eastern Church, was evinced also in his treatment of the Jews. By a bull, issued in 1442, he deprived them of most of the privileges which his predecessor had bestowed on them. He excluded them from almost every profession, forbade them to eat and drink with Christians, or to attend them medically in sickness, compelled them to wear their distinguishing badge, and declared void any bequests which Christians might make to them. His successor, the beneficent Nicolas V., who was elected a.d. 1447, pursued a wiser course. He published a decree forbidding compulsory baptisms, and warning all persons to abstain from offering insults or injuries to the Jews. During the rule of the remaining popes of the century, Calixtus III., Pius II., Paul II., Sixtus IV., Innocent VIII., and Alexander VI., the Jews seem to have been little interfered with. Odious as is the character of the last-named pope, it must be recorded to his credit that he afforded shelter to the wretched exiles whom the cruelty of Ferdinand and the Inquisition had driven out of Spain, as we shall presently record.

In the chief Italian cities also the Jews were, on the whole, well treated. The Venetians, as we have seen, allowed them to open a bank in their city; and they appear to have been the first who did so. But it may be doubted whether any large amount of gratitude was due to them on that account. It is tolerably clear that the Caorsini, Lombards, and Florentines (as the native money-lenders were called), who had hitherto engrossed the trade, exacted such enormous profits that the change to the Jews must of necessity have been a commercial advantage. It was doubtless on this account that their establishment at Venice was speedily followed by their admission to Genoa, Florence, Mantua, Verona, and Leghorn—in fact, into all the leading Italian cities—their central seat of business being fixed at Rome.

But if the amount of interest they demanded was not so exorbitant as that of the Caorsini, it was still enough to be a heavy burden on all classes. [145] Towards the end of the century the celebrated Bernardino di Feltre was stirred up to preach publicly against their exactions, and the terms on which Christians stood with them, at Piacenza. It is curious to read the language he employs, which is a strange mixture of the most truly Christian and the most utterly unchristian sentiment. He regards the Jews simply as if they had been wicked men, towards whom Christian charity must be felt and shown, but whom it is the duty of all Christian men to shun and condemn. No Christian, he says, ought to employ a Jewish physician; no Christian ought to be a guest at a Jewish feast—the risk of moral contamination is too great! 'Yet,' he adds, 'in defiance of these obstacles, which the law, no less than duty, enjoins, Christians had recently resorted in crowds to a Jewish marriage feast which lasted eight days; and it was notorious that whenever Christians were attacked by illness they resorted to a Jewish physician!' The mob, as might be expected, understood very little of his refined distinctions. They interpreted his words as an exhortation to make an attack on the Jews. They rose accordingly, and hanged and tore in pieces all they met with.[146]

He employed, however, more reasonable means of rescuing his countrymen from the clutches of the Hebrew usurer than these. He set up banks, at which a lower rate of interest was required than that demanded by the Jews, but at the same time sufficiently remunerative, provided the debts contracted were faithfully discharged. These he called Monte della Pieta. They met at first with very decided success in the chief Italian cities, and particularly in Mantua, Brescia, and Padua. In the last-named place they so engrossed the money-lending business that the Jews were obliged to close their own bank. There can be no doubt that the scheme was both commercially and philanthropically wise. Yet, after all, it did not prosper. Possibly the publicity of the dealings with Bernardino's banks was not acceptable to borrowers, who might wish the fact of their having been obliged to borrow to be kept secret. Possibly those who would fain have been customers were too deeply involved in debt to the Jews to be able to break loose from them. Possibly it was the effect of long habit, which men are ever unwilling to depart from. But, whatever may have been the cause, the scheme, after a brief period of success, began to languish, and in some places altogether failed.

It was revived later still in the century by the celebrated Girolamo Savonarola, who professed his object to be the same as that of Bernardino — rescuing his countrymen, and especially the poor, from the ruinous exactions of the Jew money-lenders, whom he denounces in the most unmeasured terms, as that 'most wicked set, the enemies of God.' Not contented with this harsh language, he obtained a decree of the State, ordering them to quit Florence within the year.

It may not be amiss, at this point of history, to inquire how far the severe language and harsh treatment with which even really good men among the Christians of the Middle Ages were wont to assail the Jews, had any reasonable justification or excuse. There were some men, as we have seen, with whom the prejudices of their brother Christians had little or no weight; who were capable of regarding the Jews as the children of their Father in heaven, and as such their brethren, though, doubtless, their erring brethren. They might rightly, in such men's eyes, be the subjects of entreaty, warning, perhaps punishment, but never of hate or contempt. But they who were thus raised above the convictions of their age were very few. And there were others — men of the highest character, whose devotion to God's service and love for their fellow-men cannot be questioned — men like Louis IX. of France, Peter of Clugny, Savonarola, Martin Luther, Cardinal Borromeo — who regarded the Jews with horror and detestation, as persons beyond the pale of charity, who were simply to be crushed and trampled out.[147] How are we to account for men like these so viewing them? Was the character of the Jews in the Middle Ages such as really to merit a condemnation so unqualified? Is the portraiture of the Jew given by our great dramatist[148] a true one? Shylock is depicted as sordid, vindictive, without mercy and without natural affection. Is he the genuine Hebrew of the sixteenth century, or the mere embodiment of blind and inveterate prejudice?

What do travellers answer when asked whether the soil of the Holy Land is waste and barren, unable to support even its sparse population? They will tell us that it is naturally rich and fertile, but has become unproductive by long neglect and abuse.[149] As it has been with the land of the Jews, so it has been with themselves. Their true national character is among the noblest—if it is not the very noblest—that the world has seen. Whatever great qualities humanity may possess, it is by men of this race that they have been exhibited in their highest development. If we ask from what nation has arisen the ablest legislator, the most far-seeing statesman, the wisest philosopher, the most chivalrous warrior, the greatest monarch, the most Heaven-inspired poet, we must answer, in every instance, From the nation of the Jews. Nor is it to individuals alone that this applies. What struggle for national independence was ever more gallant than that of the Maccabees? Which among all the countless nations, overthrown by the military genius of Rome, ever resisted so long, or with such fatal effect, her illimitable power, as the defenders of Jerusalem? But, no doubt, centuries of oppression had their effect in deteriorating the nobler, and developing the meaner, features of the Jewish character, until the Jews became at last almost—though not quite—what their persecutors believed them to be.[150] Shut out from every nobler pursuit, forbidden the career of the statesman, the soldier, the artist, the author, or the physician, except within the narrow bounds of their own despised race—they were driven to the one sordid trade of money-getting, and compelled even in that to practise the extremity of exaction and rigour, or else—subject as they were to continual lawless plunder—they could not have lived. If they were at any time disposed to show mercy, no one believed it to be anything but a subtle scheme for securing some worldly end. Treated systematically as the outcasts of humanity, what wonder if they often really became so?

FOOTNOTES:

[145] It is stated that the Jewish money-lenders demanded thirty-two and a-half per cent. on their loans, together with compound interest!

[146] The Jews were actually driven out of Ravenna in 1484, in consequence of the agitation he stirred up against them.

[147] Peter of Clugny wrote: 'If the Saracens are justly to be detested, how much more are the Jews to be execrated

and regarded with hate!' Louis IX. charged them with being in league with evil spirits to injure and destroy men. It has been affirmed that Luther treated the Jews with lenity and toleration. But, if he ever really did evince this spirit towards them, it was only at the outset of his career. Later on he was stern and merciless in his tone towards them. 'Burn their synagogues and schools,' were his words; 'break into and destroy their houses. Forbid their Rabbins, on pain of death, to teach,' etc.

[148] Shylock, it should be noted, whether a fair picture or not, of the Jews of Shakspeare's time, is at least a genuine character—a real man. But the Barabbas of Marlowe's *Jew of Malta* and the Fagin of Dickens's *Oliver Twist* are simply coarse and gross caricatures, pandering to the vulgar taste of the day.

[149] Palestine is a land 'rich in its soil, boundless in its capabilities of production, glowing in the sunshine of an almost perpetual summer—this enchanting land was indeed (what the patriarch had described it) a field which the Lord had blessed.... But Mohammedan sloth and despotism have converted it into a waste rock and desert, with the exception of some few spots, which remain to attest the veracity of the accounts formerly given of it.'—Bannister's *Holy Land*, pp. 37, 38.

[150] Every reader will remember the noble passage in *Ivanhoe*, where Bois Guilbert taunts Rebecca with the degraded character of her countrymen, and she answers him by appealing to their former greatness. 'Thou hast spoken of the Jew,' she says, 'as the persecution of such as thou has made him. Read the ancient history of the people of God, and tell me if those by whom Jehovah wrought such marvels among the nations were then a people of misers and usurers!'—*Ivanhoe*, chap. xvi.

CHAPTER XXVI
A.D. 1400-1500. THE JEWS IN SPAIN

The scenes of violence and bloodshed which had been provoked by the fanatic zeal of the Archdeacon of Ecija were a foretaste of the fearful tragedy which was to take place in Spain in the ensuing century. But it can hardly be said that he occasioned it. The evil had long been gathering, and must have broken out, sooner or later, in Spain. He may have precipitated it, but nothing more.

The main cause of the mischief was, beyond doubt, the improvidence and want of steady industry among the people. In all business transactions they were continually applying to the Jews, unable, as it seemed, to buy or sell, to sow or reap, without resorting to them. The result was the pauperizing of all classes of the community except the Jews, who continued to heap up enormous wealth.[151] The people would not believe that this was the result of their own improvidence, and that there could be no remedy for it except in persistent industry and prudence. They made repeated complaints of having been overreached and defrauded; but, when the cases were inquired into in a court of law, it was found that nothing could be proved against the alleged offenders. This only fomented the growing discontent. To all thoughtful observers it was evident that a popular convulsion could not be far distant.

Henry III. died in 1406, and was succeeded by his son John II., an infant not two years old. Early in his reign Vincentius Ferrer, a Dominican, made his appearance as an itinerant preacher in Castile and Aragon, calling on the Jews to renounce their ancient faith, and accept that of Christ. He was a man of the most ardent zeal, indefatigable energy, and burning eloquence; and the stern asceticism of his life caused him to be regarded as a saint. His fierce invectives against the impiety and obstinacy of the Jews exasperated the people against them; and it very soon became evident that there were for them two alternatives only—conversion or destruction. Vincent went from town to town, carrying a crucifix in one hand and a copy of the Mosaic Law in the other, followed everywhere by an armed rabble, who maltreated and murdered all who refused to hearken. Many of the Jews embraced, or pretended to embrace, Christianity. Many more abandoned all their worldly possessions, and fled to Barbary; some also to Portugal,[152] and other Christian States. Some would neither abjure their faith nor fly, and their descendants underwent the terrible consequences of their parents' constancy. Ferrer is said to have converted 35,000, or, according to others, 50,000 Jews. Even a Hebrew authority places it at 20,000. How many of these converts were real believers in Christ we shall have occasion subsequently to inquire.

In 1406 the old charge of insulting the Host was revived, though with some variation in the circumstances. Some Jews were accused of having bought the consecrated wafer from the sacristan of the cathedral at Segovia. They threw it into a caldron of boiling water, when it rose to the surface. Alarmed at the sight, they wrapped it in a cloth, and gave it to a Dominican friar, who informed the bishop of the occurrence. The bishop caused the Jews to be arrested and tortured. Among them was Don Meir, the king's physician. The torture not only elicited a confession of the particular crime charged on the sufferers, but of the murder of the late king by poison. Don Meir and the others were drawn and quartered at Segovia; soon after which it was discovered that the whole charge was a fabrication.

Another similar story is related about the same time. A nobleman, who bore a bitter dislike to a bishop, bribed his cook to poison him. The conspiracy was discovered, and the cook put on the rack; but he would not confess the name of his suborner. By the advice of the latter, the next time he was racked he declared it was the Jews who had bribed him. This was instantly credited; and, as he had named no particular persons as his accomplices, a great many Jews were put to death on suspicion.

In 1412 the queen-regent Catherine promulgated a series of ordinances against the Jews, equalling in severity anything that had been issued before. They were not to be physicians or surgeons; they were not to sell bread, wine, or any other provisions; they were to keep no Christian servants; were not to eat and drink with Christians, or attend Christian marriages or funerals; they were to live in the Jewries or ghettoes only, and these were to be surrounded with a high wall, having only one entrance-gate; they were to wear a carefully prescribed dress of very common material; and any Jew or Jewess who ventured to put on costly attire was liable to have the whole stripped off their backs. They were not permitted to change their place of residence, and were allowed neither to shave their beards nor cut their hair! No Christian woman was to enter the Jewish quarter, on pain of a heavy fine, if her character was respectable, or of being whipped out of it, if it was not! Finally, they were not to be smiths, carpenters, tailors, shoemakers, curriers, clothiers, or to sell any of the goods made by these, except to Jews.

In 1413 the Antipope, Benedict XIII., convened an assembly at Tortosa, for the purpose of presiding at a disputation between certain chosen advocates of Judaism on one side, and of Christianity on the other—the subjects of discussion being, whether the Messiah had already come, and what was the value of the Jewish Talmud. Considering who were to be the judges, it is no great wonder that the Jews were anxious to decline the discussion. But this they were not suffered to do. The Christian champions were Jerome of Santa Fe, Beltran, Bishop of Barcelona, and Garcia Alvares—all of them able men and converts from Judaism. Sixteen learned Talmudists appeared for the Jews. Sixty-nine meetings were held; and it is almost unnecessary once more to add that both parties claimed the victory. A bull was issued by the Pope, commanding the burning of the Talmud, and imposing fresh penalties on such Jews as remained unconverted. It appears, however, that large numbers submitted to baptism.

In 1420 the young king assumed the regal authority, and held it till 1454. During his reign the Jews seem to have been, comparatively speaking, unmolested; and, as was always the case under such circumstances, to have regained both their wealth and their political influence. In 1435 the Jews at Palma were charged with the old stock offence of crucifying children, though this time the victim was a Moor. They confessed, as usual, under torture, and, having agreed to accept baptism, were pardoned. In Toledo, in 1441, the Infante Henry, who was in rebellion against his father, being greatly in want of money to pay his troops, was advised to plunder the houses of the Jews—both those who adhered to their old creed and those who had recently been converted—as the surest and most popular mode of raising funds. He greatly approved of the counsel, and proceeded straightway to follow it, notwithstanding the opposition of the principal citizens and the clergy. The populace, we are told, followed his example. In 1445 the Jews of the same city were accused of having undermined the streets through which the procession of the Host was to pass; and one of the customary massacres would have taken place, if the authorities had not made inquiry and ascertained that the charge was wholly without foundation. Again, at Tavora, some youths, after one of their feasts, sallied forth into the streets, and slew several Jews whom they met, their excuse being that they thought the Jews were on the point of making an attack upon *them*. A similar story to that propagated at Palma was also fabricated at Valladolid of some Jews at Savona. But in no case did any of the wholesale massacres take place by which the Spanish cities were disgraced both in previous and after times.

In 1454 Henry IV. succeeded his father. His action at Toledo, thirteen years before, in plundering the Jews, caused the idea to be entertained that he would be unfavourable to them; but his conduct, when he came to the throne, did not bear out the notion. A riot having occurred in 1461 at Medina del Campo, in consequence of the preaching of an enthusiastic monk; and a number of Jews having been slain and their property pillaged, Henry put the outbreak down, and executed due justice on the rioters. He also appointed a Jew, Gaon by name, as his finance minister, and sent him to levy the taxes in the Basque provinces. But this was regarded by the Basques as an infringement of their constitutional rights. The Jew was assassinated in the streets of Tolosa; and when the king sent to require the surrender of the murderers, he received a defiant refusal, nor did he venture to take any measures against them.

It was evident that the feeling against the Jews was once more growing to the fatal height it had attained in other lands. In 1468 the Jews of Sepulveda, a town near Segovia, had, it was averred, seized on a Christian infant, carried it to a sequestered spot, and there, after barbarous ill-usage, crucified it. Their Rabbi, Solomon Picho, was declared to have been the instigator of the deed. The Bishop of Avila put the accused, sixteen in number, to the torture, and having elicited the usual confession, caused some to be burned and some hanged. But these severities did not satisfy the people of Sepulveda, who required the extermination of the Jews. They rose accordingly, and massacred all who did not save themselves by flight. Similar insurrections took place in Cordova, Jaen, Toledo, Segovia, and other cities.

The spirit thus evoked was allayed for a time—probably because Henry not only lent it no help, but was in his heart favourably inclined to the Jews. A deputation, composed of converts to Christianity and those who still professed their ancient faith, residing in Valladolid, waited on him, to ask his protection against the oppression and injustice of the partisans of his sister Donna Isabella, and were kindly received. Though no satisfaction was given them for the wrongs they had undergone, injustice for the future was restrained. When at a Cortes, held in 1469, a petition was presented to him, praying him to forbid the Jews thenceforward to farm or collect tithes, he paid no heed to it. But the spirit of persecution was checked for a time only. In 1473 it broke out again, and deluged all Andalusia with blood. A new feature was now manifested, likely to produce the gravest consequences. The storm of persecution had hitherto fallen on those only who persisted in refusing to adopt the Christian faith. But persons were now included in it who had lately become converts to the Church, and who were known by the title of the 'New Christians.' Their fidelity to their new belief was greatly suspected; and, it cannot be denied, with a good deal of reason. And, besides, these New Christians were, after all, guilty of that gravest of all Jewish offences—acquiring wealth at the expense of the old Christians. The mobs in the Andalusian cities attacked old and new Jews alike. In Jaen, the constable of the town, Franza by name, who interfered to protect them, was assassinated while hearing mass in the cathedral itself, and the pillage and murder went on unchecked. The example was soon followed in Castile. In Segovia, in 1474, Don Juan de Pachecho, wishing to provoke a rising for the execution of a political intrigue, thought the most likely mode of succeeding was by exciting an armed attack on the converted Jews, it being easy then to divert the rabble to his purpose. The insurrection was put down by the royal forces, but not before great numbers of the Jews had been slain.

Henry died in the same year, 1474, and was succeeded by his sister Isabella. Her title to the crown was doubtful, as there was a daughter of Henry's second queen, named Juana, who, if legitimate, was the rightful heir. But the whole nation seemed to have concurred in rejecting Juana's claim; and, though her cause was taken up by the King of Portugal, to whom she had given her hand, his complete defeat at Toro extinguished her hopes for ever. Five years afterwards Ferdinand succeeded to the crown of Aragon, and his union with Isabella may be said to have created anew the long extinct monarchy of Spain.

In the following year a Cortes was held at Toledo, and many laws were enacted for the government of the now united kingdoms. Among these was an ordinance, that not only should the Jews be compelled to reside within the bounds of their own Jewry or ghetto, but also that any Jew who should presume to live elsewhere should forfeit all his property, and his person be at the disposal of the king. In other respects the regulations passed were neither oppressive nor unreasonable. Within the bounds of their ghetto, all privileges which of late years they had been permitted to enjoy were allowed them. But shortly after Ferdinand's accession to the united throne of Castile and Aragon, he introduced into his dominions a new engine for the oppression of the Jews, the infamous Inquisition, the working of which produced more momentous and terrible consequences than he himself, in all likelihood, foresaw; which culminated, indeed, not only in the misery and ruin of the Jews, but in the decay and degradation of Spain herself.

This was the era of the famous Isaac Abarbanel, the favourite minister of Alphonso V., of Ferdinand and Isabella of Spain, and of Ferdinand, King of Naples. He was distinguished, not only as a statesman, but as an author. He wrote valuable commentaries on the Pentateuch and the Prophets, as well as many other works. Jacob Mantenu also, physician to Paul III., and the Latin translator of Maimonides, belongs to this century.

FOOTNOTES:

[151] A similar state of things exists in South Russia to-day.

[152] Hearing, it may be, of this, Ferrer besought permission of the King of Portugal to enter his dominions, as the messenger of Heaven. The king replied, he was welcome to come, but he must first prove his mission by putting on a crown of red-hot iron! Ferrer declined to avail himself of this offer!

CHAPTER XXVII
A.D. 1400-1500. THE JEWS
IN SPAIN—*continued*

The Inquisition, introduced into Spain by Ferdinand, with the consent of Isabella,[153] was not a new institution. It had been established in France early in the thirteenth century, the object then being to compel the return of the Albigenses to the orthodox faith. It had worked terrible woe to that unhappy people; but two hundred and fifty years afterwards the heresy had so nearly died out, that the Inquisition would have died along with it, if it had not been that the outcry respecting the New Christians, as they were called—that is the recent converts to Christianity—once more set the hateful machinery in operation. The height to which the persecution of the Jews had risen in the fifteenth century had left them no alternative but apostasy or death. It is no wonder that large numbers of the Jews preferred the former. It is said that no less than thirty-five thousand persons had been induced to accept baptism by the preaching of Vincent Ferrer alone. For a time the clergy felt overwhelmed with joy at this signal triumph; but after a while grave suspicions of the sincerity of these new converts began to be felt. Outwardly, no doubt, they conformed to the requirements of the Church; but it was suspected that they still continued to observe in secret the Jewish ritual.

Three inquisitors were appointed, Torquemada, Juglar, and D'Avila; and their first act was to put forth an edict, in which they declared it to be the duty of all faithful Christians, without paying any regard to rank or condition, to accuse to the tribunal any whom they knew to be open professors but secret enemies of Christ. Any who did not do so became themselves amenable to the law for their criminal silence. To facilitate such accusations, a manifesto was issued, in which various proofs were mentioned by which a 'secret Jew' might be detected. We learn from it that a man might be accounted as a concealed Jew if, among many similar evidences, he—

1. Put on clean clothes, or had a clean table-cloth on the Saturday, or dispensed with a fire on the Friday night.

2. If he washed the blood from meat, or examined the knife before slaying an animal.

3. If, on the Day of Atonement, he asked forgiveness of those whom he had offended, or put his hands on his children's heads to bless them, without making the sign of the cross.

4. If he gave his children Jewish names.[154]

5. If he ate the same meat as Jews, or sat down to table with them. If, when dying, he turned his face to the wall, or let any one else turn it. If he washed a corpse with warm water. If he spoke approvingly of the dead (such person being a Jew), or made lamentation for him, or caused a body to be buried in virgin soil, etc.

If it were not that these enactments were followed up by the most barbarous and insatiable cruelties, it would be difficult to read this extraordinary catalogue of offences without a smile. But all disposition to mirth vanishes when we remember what ensued. Great numbers of arrests, we are told, were made—the practice of keeping the accuser's name a profound secret rendering it easy to indulge malevolence without the risk of exposure. The accused, not being told the exact nature or details of the charges against them, were unable to disprove them; and, not being confronted with the witnesses, could not expose their falsehood. Both witnesses and accused, again, were frequently put to the severest tortures, under the pressure of which they made confessions which they were not allowed to retract. In short, it was wholly impossible for any one to escape condemnation when it was the wish or the interest of the inquisitors to condemn him; and it is no wonder that the list of their victims should have extended to a length so fearful.

Fearful indeed it is to read. During the eighteen years of Torquemada's inquisitorship, more than ten thousand persons were burned alive; more than six thousand corpses, of persons found guilty after their deaths, were dragged from their graves and fastened to the stakes, along with the living victims; while nearly one hundred thousand were stripped of all their possessions, and sentenced to life-long imprisonment.[155]

All classes of men were shocked and alarmed at these dreadful scenes. The Cortes appealed to the Pope, who made a feeble attempt to interfere, but soon desisted; while, in Saragossa, a conspiracy was organized, and Arbues d'Avila, one of the three inquisitors, was assassinated in the cathedral. But this did not benefit the unhappy Jews. Whether guilty or not of the act, all men considered them so, and left them to what they regarded as the just penalty of their crime.

Thus far the persecution had been directed entirely to the *conversos,* or New Christians. Such of the Jews as had refused to abandon their faith had been left uninjured; nor is it unlikely that they considered this as being the just reward of their constancy. But their turn was now to come. Ferdinand and Isabella, who had at last succeeded in reducing the whole of Spain to their sovereignty, resolved that thenceforth none should breathe the air of that land who denied the Christian faith. In 1492 they issued the memorable decree, commanding all Jews to renounce their creed or depart from Spain. It was dated March 30th, and allowed them four months in which to prepare for their departure. Any Jews who presumed to linger in the country after the expiration of that date, or to return to it at any future time, were to be liable to the penalty of death, and the forfeiture of all their goods. Any persons who publicly or privately sheltered or protected any of the proscribed race, after the 31st of July, were to be punished by the confiscation of their entire property.

The blow fell like a thunderbolt on the unhappy people. It has been several times remarked that, considering the irreconcilable enmity entertained towards them, and the incessant wrongs they underwent, it could have been no great privation to be exiled from lands which contained none but bitter and merciless enemies. But they do not understand human nature who would so argue. Man is like a creeping plant, which puts out its tendrils to clasp the objects nearest to it; and, though these may be rough bark or barren rock, it cannot be torn away from them without resistance and pain. And if this was applicable to the Jews in all countries, it was especially true as regarded Spain. There, for centuries, they had dwelt, peaceful, prosperous, and happy. While their brethren in other lands underwent cruel insult and wrong, they had been protected against violence by wise and just rulers. Only recently had the hand of violence been raised against them; and they might surely hope that it might be withdrawn ere long, when calmer reason again bore sway.

An attempt was made to induce the king to forego his purpose. The celebrated Isaac Abarbanel[156] was at the time high in his confidence and favour. He threw himself at Ferdinand's feet, and offered, in the name of his people, no less than 30,000 ducats, as the price of their continuance in Spain. So large a sum tempted Ferdinand, who was at all times avaricious, and was at that moment greatly in need of money. He wavered, and might perhaps have revoked his edict, if Torquemada, who had heard of the offer, had not burst into the presence-chamber, holding a crucifix in his hand. 'Behold,' he cried, 'Him whom Judas sold for thirty pieces of silver! Sell Him again, if you will, and render an account of the bargain to God!' Isabella also took part against the Jews. It may well be, that the notion of being bribed to forego her duty roused an indignation which she would not otherwise have felt. Any way, the offer was rejected, and the miserable Jews had to set about making the best provision they could against the approaching day of exile. They were allowed to sell their landed property and houses, but only, of course, at an enormous disadvantage. Bernaldes states that he saw Jews give a house in exchange for an ass, and a vineyard for a small bale of cloth, purchasers continually holding off from completing a bargain, which they knew they must ultimately get on their own terms. They were forbidden to carry away with them gold or silver; but we are told that they contrived to secrete large quantities of it in the saddles and halters of their horses. Some even swallowed it, and it is said, in some instances, to the amount of thirty ducats! The rich Jews paid the expenses of their poorer brethren,[157] practising towards each other the greatest charity.

At the beginning of July, they set out on their mournful journey to the seaports, old and young, rich and poor, a long and melancholy *cortége*. The Rabbins, we are told, encouraged them, and engaged musicians to play, and bade the boys and girls sing, so as to keep up the spirits of the wayfarers. But the mirth must have been forced and hollow. Their fathers could not sing the Lord's song while compelled to dwell in a strange land—how should they sing it when forced to leave their own?

There is considerable difference in the estimate made by historians of the numbers that went into exile. Mariana reckoned it at 800,000. Others place it much lower; but at the least calculation it must have reached some hundreds of thousands. An immense concourse assembled at Barcelona, Valencia, Carthagena, Port Maria, and Gibraltar. Vessels had been provided at all those ports, whence they were transported to Italy, or various places on the coast of Africa. The miseries endured during the voyage, and after the landing had been effected, exceed all power of description. Some of the vessels took fire; others were so overloaded that they sank. Many were wrecked on barren places along the African shore, and died of cold and hunger. Some captains purposely prolonged their voyages, in order that the provisions might run short, and their passengers be obliged to purchase water and food of them at any price they might choose to exact. On board one vessel, a pestilential disease broke out. The captain landed all the emigrants on a desert island, where many perished of famine. Another party was forced to go ashore at an uninhabited spot, where a large portion of them were devoured by wild beasts. Those who reached Fez, in Morocco, were not allowed to enter the town, but were compelled to encamp on the sands, suffering the most grievous privations, and exposed to the brutal insults of the natives.[158] A Sallee pirate allured a number of boys on board his vessel, promising to bestow some provisions on them, and then carried them off before the faces of their parents, who stood imploring and shrieking for mercy on the shore, to sell them as slaves at a distant port.

Those that were conveyed to Italy were somewhat less harshly treated. The captain of a vessel bound for Genoa, passing along the African coast, saw a number of naked wretches, who apparently had been cast by the sea upon it. On inquiry he found that these were a number of Jewish exiles, who had been barbarously compelled to land there. He took them on board, made them some clothes out of sailcloth, and conveyed them to Genoa. There they were permitted to land; but were met by priests carrying bread in one hand and a crucifix in the other, nor would they bestow the former on them until they had consented to accept the latter also. Nine crowded vessels reached the Bay of Naples; but disease, caused by the hardships and privations of the voyage, was raging amongst the passengers. The infection was speedily communicated to the city, and 20,000 persons are reported to have died in consequence. In Rome, even the selfish nature of Alexander VI. was moved at the recital of their sufferings. He not only gave them shelter in his own dominions, but wrote to all the Italian States, desiring them to extend to the Jewish exiles the same privileges which had been enjoyed by their resident brethren.[159]

FOOTNOTES:

[153] It was with great difficulty that this was obtained. Isabella, though a dutiful daughter of the Church, had a superior intellect and a tender heart; and both revolted against the proposed measure. Torquemada, who had been her confessor, was obliged to appeal to a promise she had made him, years before, to extirpate heresy, if she ever could. Even then, her assent was most reluctantly given.

[154] By a previous law of Henry II., he had become punishable if he gave his children *Christian* names. It must have been a hard matter to know what to call them.

[155] The wholesale butchery of the Autos da Fé, as these executions were called, is one of their most shocking features. On the 4th of November, 1481, three hundred Jews were burned in Seville, and in other parts of the same province two thousand more. In Saragossa the two surviving inquisitors avenged the assassination of their colleague by two hundred deaths at the stake.

[156] Don Isaac Abarbanel was born at Lisbon in 1437, and early gained the notice of Alphonso V. He was obliged to

leave Portugal suddenly in 1482, having been suspected of taking part in Bragazza's conspiracy against John II. He was kindly welcomed by Ferdinand and Isabella, who made him their Minister of Finance. In 1492, he was obliged to quit Spain along with his countrymen. He found refuge at Naples, where he was employed by Ferdinand and Alphonso II. He shared the exile of the latter monarch, and removed to Venice, where he died.

[157] The charge of sordid indifference to the sufferings of others has always been made against the mediæval Jews; nor can it be denied that there is truth in the allegation. But it was only towards the Christians that this was displayed. To their own countrymen they have in all ages been generous and charitable in the extreme. Be it remembered what kind of charity had been shown *them* by their Christian brethren, and that *they* had not been taught 'to do good unto them that persecute you.' When the Jews at Rome were unwilling to receive their exiled brethren of Spain, Alexander VI. expressed the utmost surprise. 'This is the first time,' he said, 'that I ever heard of a Jew not having compassion for a Jew.'

[158] Some of the stories related of the atrocities perpetrated on these miserable wretches are too shocking for repetition. They are related by several historians, but I think it better, for the credit of human nature, to suppress them.

[159] It must be noted, however, that, although Alexander showed compassion to the fugitives, he made them pay a heavy price for his protection of them, and also bestowed on Ferdinand the title of 'the Most Catholic,' in requital of the banishment of the Jews from his dominions.

CHAPTER XXVIII
A.D. 1400-1500. THE JEWS IN PORTUGAL

No mention has hitherto been made of the Jews dwelling in Portugal. Little is said respecting them by historians; and the idea has in consequence been entertained that they were few in number, and had little influence in the affairs of the country. But that is a mistake. They settled early in various parts of Portugal, and under the rule of the first Portuguese kings bore an important part in its concerns. In the reign of Sancho I., in 1190, a Jew, Don Solomon Jachia, was made a field-marshal, and commanded the Portuguese army. In 1248, Sancho II. appointed so many Jews to public offices that the Pope of the day, Gregory IX., remonstrated with him on the subject, and requested that Christians might be chosen for the various posts of receivers and farmers of the revenue, which then were generally occupied by Jews, to the oppression and injury of Christian men. We are told that, in requital of the royal protection granted them, the Jews furnished an anchor and a cable of sixty fathoms' length to every king's vessel which left port.

The same favour was continued by subsequent monarchs. In 1289, the clergy laid a complaint before Pope Nicolas IV. against King Dennis, that he appointed Jews to the highest offices in the State; the Chief Rabbi Judah being his High Treasurer and Minister of Finance. The consequence was they stated, that he permitted his countrymen to dispense with the payment of tithe due from them, and also to lay aside their distinguishing badge. But the complaint seems to have been without foundation. When, at Evora, in 1325 sumptuary laws were enacted respecting dress, no exceptions were made in favour of the Jews; and, unless a composition entered into with the Jews of Braganza, accepting a fixed sum in lieu of the annual taxes, can be regarded as such, no special favour was shown them.

Alphonso IV., in 1340, remitted the extraordinary impositions which, from time to time, had been exacted of them, commuting them for a sum which, though *per se* large, was a great relief to them. His successor, Ferdinand, in 1371 ordered that all the privileges which had been granted by his predecessors to the Jews should be confirmed. He had a Jew, Don Judah, for his treasurer. In 1389, John I., at the suit of Moses, his physician, gave his sanction to the bull of Clement VI., which had been confirmed by the newly elected Pope, Boniface IX., granting the Jews licence to celebrate their feasts, and practise the rites of their religion without interruption from any. In short, up to the date of the accession of John II., in 1481, though laws were passed from time to time, imposing penalties and restrictions on the Jews, which we in the present day should consider harsh and unfair, there was nothing which amounted to persecution.[160]

On the accession of John II., in 1481, he held a Cortes at Evora, when great complaints were made of the luxury in which the Jews indulged, and the display they made of their riches. They rode splendidly caparisoned horses, wore silk doublets, carried jewel-hilted swords, entered churches, where they made a mock of the worship in progress; above all, refused to wear the badge by which they were distinguished. Jewish artisans, too—cobblers, tinkers, and the like—roamed about the country, making their way into houses, while the men were engaged at work in the fields, and perverting the women. The king replied to these various complaints, promising to restrain the indulgence in splendid apparel, and to oblige the Jews to wear their badge; but adding that, as regards other offences, if it could be proved that they had committed them, the law would punish them.

In 1491, when the expulsion from Spain took place, large numbers of the exiles found a refuge in Portugal. It was the most likely spot for them to select. There was no long and perilous sea-voyage to be encountered, and the similarity of language and customs of the two countries made the change less harsh and painful. But though John permitted the fugitives to find a shelter in his dominions, it was only for a brief interval, and upon very stern conditions. He required that all persons, excepting children at the breast, should pay the sum of eight crusadoes (19s. 4d.) each, in return for which they received a certificate, entitling them to reside eight months in the kingdom. At the expiration of that time, the king engaged to provide vessels, on reasonable terms, to convey them to any land they might select. Those who could not pay the crusadoes, or lingered in Portugal after the prescribed time, were to become the slaves of the king.[161] Upon these terms as many as 20,000 families, amounting probably to more than 100,000 persons, crossed into Portugal, with the intention probably of quitting its inhospitable shores as speedily as possible. But the eight months passed, and large numbers still lingered. Some were doubtless too poor to pay for a passage, for which exorbitant prices were charged. The king had, indeed, ordered that no more than a reasonable sum should be asked, but his commands were slackly and carelessly carried out, and complaint would have been worse than useless. Many were terrified by the tales of barbarities practised on their countrymen by the savage inhabitants of the African coast, and many had been enfeebled by the pestilence which had broken out among them. No sooner had the eight months expired than the penalty was enforced, and the whole of the loiterers became the slaves of the king. Those who were young and able-bodied were forcibly baptized, and then carried off to colonize the island of St. Thomas, in the Gulf of Guinea, which had recently become a Portuguese possession.

In 1495, John was succeeded by Emmanuel, known in history as 'the Fortunate.' His succession appeared at first to promise the miserable Jews some respite from their sufferings. He revoked the edict under which such as had remained in the kingdom became slaves. He refused a large sum of money which had been presented to him by some wealthy Jews, and professed his determination of treating them with equity and mercy.

Unhappily, the gleam of sunshine soon passed away, and was succeeded by a fiercer tempest than any that had yet darkened their skies. In an unhappy hour Emmanuel sued for the hand of the Infanta Isabella, daughter of the Catholic sovereigns of Spain; and they would not consent to the marriage, except on the condition that their son-in-law should banish the Jews from Portugal, as they had banished them from Spain. We may believe that there was a struggle in his mind, for he was evidently inclined to be compassionate towards the unfortunate race, which he had already befriended. But what, after all, were a few thousands of wretched Jews, when compared with the fulfilment of his hopes? Nay, he would win the approval of his lady-love by doing even more than had been required of him. He would win her favour at once, and that of Heaven also, by his fulfilment of their wishes. He issued a proclamation from Muja, ordering all the Jews still within his dominions to embrace the Christian faith within the space of three months, or to depart from Portugal. Three ports were at first named—Lisbon Oporto, and Setubal—from any of which the Jews might embark; but subsequently this order was revoked, and Lisbon was named as the only place of embarkation. It is probable that Emmanuel expected, after the great reluctance which the Jews had manifested, on a recent occasion, to quit their present place of abode for unknown and unfriendly regions, that the greater part, at all events, would choose baptism rather than deportation. When he found that this was not the case, but that great numbers were resolute to depart, and were making the needful preparations for their voyage, he was greatly disconcerted. The glory of making converts to the Church would be denied him, and he would lose a vast number of wealthy and valuable subjects. He resolved not to forego these advantages without at least making another effort to secure them. He despatched a secret order that all children under fourteen should be separated from their parents, and brought up in the Christian faith. This was not to be carried into effect until the day of embarkation came, so that there would be no time left for disputing or evading the decrees. But the king's intention was by some error divulged; and, lest the Jews should contrive to defeat it, it was put into immediate execution. Such scenes of horror ensued as imagination cannot picture. It was the repetition, on a larger scale, of the massacre at Bethlehem. Children were dragged forcibly from the grasp of their parents; infants torn from their mothers' breasts, to undergo what they regarded as worse then death. Many, in the distraction of their agony, flung their children into the wells and rivers, or slew themselves with their own hands. [162] One miserable mother threw herself at the feet of the king, as he was riding to church—to *church*! Great God of Mercy, that men should dare to bring such deeds into Thy very house, for Thine approval! She cried out that six of her seven children had already been taken from her—would he not spare her youngest to her? The courtiers mocked at her misery. The king bade his attendants remove her from his path—'the poor bitch,' as he expressed it, 'robbed of her whelps!'—whether with her petition granted or not, we are not told. But the people were not so deaf to the common instincts of humanity as their monarch. They assisted the Jews to conceal their children, and the inhuman command was only partially carried out. Nevertheless, this last deadly blow had gone further to break the hearts of the Jews than all their previous sufferings. On condition of receiving back their children, and that the Inquisition should not be introduced into Portugal for twenty years to come,[163] many of those who had hitherto resisted all attempts to proselytize them consented to receive baptism. The more steadfast spirits, whom no amount of suffering could subdue, were either shipped off to foreign lands or remained behind after the appointed day, and became the slaves of Emmanuel.

It must not be supposed that these acts of bigotry and pitiless cruelty were done with the universal consent of the Portuguese people. The rabble, indeed, in every land can at all times be stirred up to hunt down and oppress those who differ from themselves on almost any subject, without reflection and without remorse; yet, even among them, as we have seen, the natural feelings of compassion could not be wholly stifled. But among the more educated and thoughtful classes there were many who not only disapproved the act of their sovereign, but openly expressed their dissatisfaction. Bishop Osorio has plainly recorded the view which he and others took of it. 'Some of the king's counsellors,' he says, 'were of opinion that the Jews ought not to be driven away, since it was notorious that the Pope himself permitted them to reside in his dominions. Other Christian princes in Italy, following his example—as well as some in Germany, Hungary, and other European States,—granted them the same liberty, and allowed them to practise various trades and professions. As for converting them to the Church, banishment would be less likely than any other step to bring that about. The Jews would carry with them their perverse dispositions. *Cœlum non animum mutant qui trans mare currunt*—a change of residence would have no effect in producing a change of conviction. Nay, to send them over to Africa would be to destroy what hope at present existed of their conversion. Living among Christians, they might be influenced by the Christian example set them [alas! what kind of Christian example *had* been set them?] and adopt the true faith. But, mingling with blind and superstitious Mahometans, how could they learn any good? Again, to put the matter on wholly different grounds, it would be most injurious to the State to send out of the land a people possessed of abundant wealth, which would then enrich their enemies.' But the words of Divine and human wisdom alike failed to produce any effect on the infatuated king and his advisers, and the fatal policy was persisted in.

During this century many learned and able writers belonging to the Hebrew race have transmitted their names to posterity. Mention has been made in the previous chapter of Isaac Abarbanel, divine, philosopher, and historian, the most celebrated Jew of his age. Contemporary with him were Isaac Aboab, author of commentaries, essays, and sermons; David ben Solomon Jachia, grammarian, poet, and Talmudist; Judah, Joseph, and Samuel Abarbanel, sons of the renowned Isaac, the first-named also an author of repute; Solomon ben Virga, the historian; David ben Joseph Jachia, philosopher, grammarian, and poet; and many others.

During this century printing-presses were introduced into Portugal by two Jews, Eliezer and Izarba, by whom some beautiful editions of the Pentateuch and the Targum of Onkelos were produced. Hebrew presses were also set up about the same time in many of the great Italian cities.

FOOTNOTES:

[160] Thus, the Jews were compelled to live in their Jewry; they could not have Christian servants; they were prohibited from entering the houses of Christians, unless they were accompanied by two Christians; they were not allowed to wear silk dresses; they were not allowed to collect the revenue of the Church. But no one could do them wrong without their obtaining redress; there was no hint of

confiscating their wealth; and they were free to practise any trade or profession.

[161] Except smiths and armourers, who were permitted to remain in the country if they chose.

[162] The corpses of these were publicly burnt, as a token of the anger of Heaven against *their* wickedness!

[163] The converts also stipulated that, when the Inquisition was set up, its judicial proceedings should be so far modified that accused persons should be confronted with the witnesses against them; and, in case of condemnation, their entire property should not be taken from their families.

CHAPTER XXIX
A.D. 1500-1600. THE JEWS IN ITALY

The Jews had now been expelled from England, France, parts of Germany and Central Europe, Russia, Spain, and Portugal.[164] They were also shut out from Holland and the Low Countries, these being subject to the control of the Empire. It does not appear that they had ever established themselves in Sweden, Denmark, or Scotland, to any great extent. In fact, the only European countries in which they continued to reside in any considerable numbers, at this period, were Italy, Poland, and Turkey. It was chiefly in the East and in Northern Africa, under the rule of Mahometan princes, that they found a refuge. We shall speak first of the residents in Europe during this century, and then proceed to record the fortunes of their brethren who had migrated to the East.

They were received, as we have seen, with more kindness than might have been expected in Italy. Many of the Popes were far-sighted enough to perceive that, by expelling the Jews from their dominions, they were simply transferring capital and intelligence to other countries.[165] Leo X., in 1513, checked the zeal of certain preachers, who were inveighing against the Jewish usurers in Rome. He had no mind to have popular tumults excited, which might oblige him to drive out men whose residence in the city was so advantageous to him. His successor, Clement VII., adopted a similar policy. When he heard of the persecution in Portugal, a.d. 1523, undergone by the New Christians (as those Jews were called who were recent converts to the Church), he not only sent an invitation to them to come and live in his dominions, but intimated that he should not inquire what had happened to them previously in Portugal. It need not be said that great numbers availed themselves of his offer. Paul III., 1539, espoused their cause still more openly. He would not permit the Inquisition to continue its persecuting and bloody work within the Papal States. Whatever offences might have been charged against the Jews in their own land, when they crossed the confines of his, a full amnesty was granted them. Especially this was the case in the rising city of Ancona. Entire freedom of trade was permitted, no inquiries being made as to any man's creed. There was complete equality of taxation. No one was compelled to wear any distinguishing badge. We are told that, in consequence of these measures, Ancona grew rapidly in population and wealth. It was doubtless in consequence of this special favour that Cardinal Sadolet complained, at Avignon, of the extraordinary favour shown to the Israelites; and we learn that, later in his reign, Paul issued a bull, annulling the decrees he had made in their favour, and requiring that converts to the Church should be separated from their relatives.

Ten years afterwards Julius III. confirmed the privileges which his predecessors had granted; indeed, he went further. Considering that the Reformation was making dangerous progress in Italy, he thought it necessary to set up the Inquisition in Rome. But he especially exempted the Jews of Ancona from its supervision. And, as regards the other Jews in his dominions, he gave the most stringent directions to his legates and cardinals to show the most complete toleration to their religious opinions and observances. They were to make no inquiry as to what they professed, or what they might formerly have professed—this last promise being obviously intended to meet the case of those Jewish exiles who, in their native country, had been induced to make a nominal profession of Christianity, which they had now laid aside.

His tolerant treatment of them, however, was subjected to a severe trial. A Franciscan friar, one Corneglio of Montalcino, had become a convert to Judaism, and forthwith was possessed with a spirit of proselytism, which drove him openly to preach the falsehood of Christianity in the very streets of Rome! He was seized, and inquiry made as to the cause of his apostasy. Fortunately for the Jews, this was alleged to be the study of the Talmud, not the personal influence of any Jew. Of the Talmud, accordingly, the penalty was exacted. It was ordered to be publicly burned in Rome and other Italian cities. The Jews, who had lived in terror of a furious popular outbreak or a stern papal decree, were allowed to escape scot free—an act of mercy which is gratefully recorded by one of their Rabbins.

But it was different when Paul IV. succeeded to the pontificate, a man of arrogant and impetuous character, who carried intolerance, it might be said, to the highest pitch of which it is capable.[166] He was as stern in his demeanour to the Jews as he was to the Reformers. He renewed all the hostile edicts that had been in force against them in the time of his predecessors. He prohibited them from holding real property, and compelled them to sell what they were possessed of within six months,—of course at a ruinous loss. He debarred them from trading in corn, or any of the necessaries of life, though he allowed them the privilege of dealing in old clothes, with which traffic they have been so generally associated in the popular fancy. He ordered all their synagogues but one to be destroyed. He was the first to shut them up in the Ghetto, where, for centuries afterwards, they were forced to live. He obliged them again to wear a distinctive dress—the men yellow hats, the women yellow hoods—to abstain from work on the Sunday, to keep from all intercourse with Christians, and especially from attending them as physicians, and to pay a tax for the instruction in the Christian faith of any Jews who were inclined to embrace it.

His rule, however, only lasted for four years, and Pius IV., who succeeded him in 1559, somewhat, though not very greatly, relaxed the sternness of his predecessor's policy. He maintained the enforced residence within the Ghetto, but he enlarged and improved it, and forbade the exorbitant rents which the owners of houses had hitherto exacted. He removed several restrictions on their trade, and permitted them to hold real property up to the value of 1500 ducats. He allowed friendly intercourse between them and their Christian fellow-subjects, and, though he would not dispense with the cap, which was one of their distinguishing badges, he changed its colour from yellow to the less remarkable one of black.

Pius V., 1566, a man of austere and sombre character, revived in a great measure the harshness of Paul IV. He banished the Jews from all the cities in his domains, except Rome and Ancona, and revived most of the severities with which Pius IV. had dispensed. He seems to have tolerated the presence of the Jews at all, only because by that time it had come to be generally understood that to expel them from any country was to destroy its commercial prosperity. There was little change in their treatment when Gregory XIII. followed, a.d. 1572. He promulgated a bull, which he caused to be fixed at the entrance of the Ghetto, which prohibited the reading of the Talmud, and required all Jews who were more than twelve years of age to appear periodically, for the purpose of listening to sermons preached for their special conversion. What effect these had in producing the desired result, we are not informed.

In 1585, however, Sixtus V. assumed the pontificate—a man of far higher character and more commanding mind than any of his predecessors during the present century. His mode of dealing with the Jews was at once humane and statesmanlike. He swept away with a stroke of his pen the vexatious and frivolous restrictions which had been imposed on them; he gave them free access to, and unrestrained residence in, all the cities of his dominions; he allowed them to carry on whatever trade they might prefer; he ordered the full toleration of their religion; subjected them to the same civil tribunals and the same taxes as their Christian fellow-subjects. He also limited the amount of usury which they were permitted to exact to eighteen per cent.

After his death, in 1590, there was a succession of Popes who vacated the papal chair almost immediately after occupying it.[167] Clement VIII., who was elected in 1592, confirmed the bull of Pius V., by which they were banished out of all the papal cities except Rome and Ancona; but to these he added Avignon, where they have since resided, with full liberty of holding their religious belief and maintaining their form of worship.

In the other Italian States their condition during this century appears to have been quite as good—somewhat better, indeed, than it was at Rome. In Florence they were kindly received, and so well protected by the laws, that we are told it was a favourite saying in that city, that 'a man might as well insult the Grand Duke himself as a Jew.'[168] In Venice they were equally in favour. They had already, in the previous century, obtained permission to set up a bank in the city, the Senate being aware of the commercial advantages obtained by the residence of the Jews among them. They disapproved the step taken by the Spanish and Portuguese kings, and themselves employed Jews on missions of importance, as for instance Abarbanel, to negotiate a treaty with Portugal; and in 1589, another Jew, Daniel Rodriguez, to put down some troubles in Dalmatia, which he successfully accomplished. In Livorno (Leghorn), which the Medici in the latter part of this century took under their special protection, designing it to become a great mart of European trade, a quarter was especially assigned to the Spanish and Portuguese exiles, who flocked thither in great numbers. It was, indeed, declared to be a Jewish colony, and it has continued to flourish from that day to the present time. The Spanish language is still spoken by the Hebrew population, and the Mosaic ritual is maintained, says a modern writer, in great splendour.

At Ferrara, the Spanish and Portuguese emigrants were received with the same favour, and the like privileges, which had been accorded by other Italian princes. Their numbers were so great, that the duke was induced, probably by popular clamour, to revive an old law, requiring them to wear a small yellow circle on the breast. From the same cause, popular pressure, he was obliged in 1551 to dismiss the whole of the Hebrew population from his realm, in consequence of a widespread, though it would seem unfounded, belief that they had brought the plague into Ferrara. They were, however, soon permitted to return. Many Jews also settled at Bologna, Cremona, Modena, Mantua, Padua, and other large towns, where they were kindly received.

At Naples only of the Italian cities they were not permitted to find a home. In the first instance, as the reader has learned, a considerable number of the Spanish exiles had found refuge in that city, where they had been received in a friendly manner. But the invasion of Charles VIII. of France exposed them to fresh persecution. Wearied out by their endless trials, they lost heart at last, and consented to embrace the Christian faith. But, as in the other instances, the conversion was only nominal, and the danger had no sooner passed than the pseudo-converts returned to their former profession. A few years subsequently Gonsalvo de Cordova took possession of Naples in the name of the King of Spain. He raised the question as to whether they ought not to be driven out of the country, which had now become part of the Spanish dominions. But the idea had now got possession of most people's minds, that to expel the Jews from any country was to do it serious injury. He therefore proposed to introduce the Inquisition, which would retain the Jews in the land, but compel them to keep to their newly made profession. This, however, did not please the Neapolitans, who rose in insurrection, and the government were fain to compromise the matter by expelling the Jews; though it is affirmed by some of the Jewish writers (as, for example, Orobio de Castro) that these stern measures were adopted only so far as the Sephardim (or Spanish Jews) were concerned.

In this century great numbers of Hebrew printing-presses were set up in Italy, which were under the management of learned Jews. Among these was the celebrated Abraham Usque, by whom the well-known Bible of Ferrara, a Spanish version of the Old Testament, was printed. Hebrew presses were also erected at Cremona, Leghorn, Padua, Genoa, Rimini, and Verona, as well as the central city of Rome. The renowned Daniel Bomberg of Antwerp established himself at Venice in 1516, and his works attained great celebrity. He also published the first complete edition of the Talmud, and the first Rabbinical Bible. To this age also belongs Rabbi Joseph, the historian of the French Crusades and the sufferings of the Jews in Castile, Asarja de Rossi, and Abraham Portaleone.

FOOTNOTES:

[164] It would, however, be a mistake to suppose that they were not to be met with in those countries. Even in England, though the law forbade any settlement, Jews were occasionally to be found, whose presence was tolerated. This was still more the case in France and Germany; while in Spain and Portugal great numbers remained, whose profession of Christianity was very widely known to be a mere pretence. Of them we shall speak in the next chapter.

[165] Sultan Bajazet was shrewd enough to apprehend this. When he heard of the banishment of the Jews by Ferdinand,

he exclaimed: 'A wise king this, who impoverishes his own kingdom to enrich mine!'

[166] Paul IV. was the Pope whose overbearing dealings with Queen Elizabeth precipitated the rupture with the English Church. He was also the author of the well-known *Index* of prohibited books.

[167] Urban VIII., Gregory XIV., and Innocent IX.

[168] A remarkable instance of the esteem in which they were held in Florence is to be found in the quarrel between Florence and Milan in 1414. The Florentines, considering that they had cause of complaint against the Duke of Milan, sent a Jewish banker, named Valori, as an ambassador to him. The duke refused to receive a Jew as an envoy, which the Florentines so highly resented that they declared war against him.

CHAPTER XXX
A.D. 1500-1600. THE JEWS IN PORTUGAL, SPAIN, AND HOLLAND

The Jews having been publicly expelled from Portugal and Spain, it might be thought that there was an end of their history, so far as those two countries are concerned. So, doubtless, there would have been, had the expulsion been a complete one. But it was notorious that, though they had been nominally driven out, great numbers remained, who, though they called themselves Christians, were in reality Jews, and nothing but Jews. Miserable as was the condition of those whose sufferings have been described in the previous chapters, it may be doubted whether those who stayed behind were not more wretched still. True, they had escaped the dreaded severance from home and country; they might still dwell among the familiar scenes of youth and manhood; they had not undergone the horrors of the outward voyage, and the landing among barbarous and inhospitable strangers. But there was the self-reproach and shame of a false profession of faith; there was the necessity of complying with forms and observances which in their heart they hated; there was the continued dread of detection and ruin. They knew themselves to be the objects of continual suspicion, that keen and merciless eyes were ever upon them, and that on the slightest evidence of any open recurrence to the worship which they still secretly rendered, the fearful scenes, still fresh in their memory, would be renewed.

It was not long before these anticipations were fulfilled. On Easter Day, 1506, a fierce and sanguinary outbreak occurred in Lisbon, which illustrates only too faithfully the state of public feeling in that day towards the New Christians—which had now become the customary designation of the Jews. Its immediate cause was an insult offered to a famous miraculous crucifix, which had been brought out of the cathedral into the great square. The plague had broken out in the town, the season was unusually dry, and the pestilence was aggravated by the want of water. It was hoped that through the aid of the image some help might be sent from above. On a sudden, while the eyes of all were anxiously fixed on it, the features of the sculptured Christ were seen to smile. The people all broke out into expressions of admiring thankfulness, except one man, who declared that the smile had been caused by a stream of light let in by a lamp through the back of the figure. He was one of the New Christians, and the hollowness of his profession had already been suspected. The Dominicans denounced him as an apostate, and he was instantly struck down and slain. The mob followed up this deed of violence by attacking and slaying all the countrymen of the offender whom they encountered. The monks incited them to further excesses, promising (it is said by a Jewish historian) that whoever should murder a Jew would not have to pass more than one hundred days in purgatory, let his offences be what they might. The rabble, thus incited, assailed, gutted, and burned the houses of all the Jews in the town; men, women, and children were everywhere massacred; those who had fled into the churches for sanctuary were torn from the altars, dragged out, and burned. For three days the carnage went on unchecked. At the end of that time King Emmanuel, who had been absent at Abrantes, returned to Lisbon. He sent a body of troops into the town sufficient to quell the disturbance; the ringleaders of the outbreak were arrested and hanged; and the magistrates, who had shown their incompetency to deal with the emergency, removed from office. Such of the New Christians as had escaped the murderous hands of the mob again passed under the protection of the law. Yet they could not but have felt like men dwelling near the crater of some volcanic mountain, which might at any moment burst forth in torrents of burning lava, and overwhelm them utterly; and it is worthy of notice that, although the rioters were sternly punished for their lawless violence, no reparation was made to the Jews—not even an expression of regret was uttered for the unprovoked and cruel wrongs they had undergone. It is passing strange that they should have still clung to a land so unkindly, and still more strange that those who had quitted it for other countries, where at least life and property were secure, should have been anxious to return to it.

Yet this did occur. When Charles V., the grandson of Ferdinand and Isabella, succeeded in 1519 to the throne of Spain, some of the Jewish exiles sent a deputation to him, requesting permission to reoccupy their ancient homes, free from the perpetual and pitiless interference of the Inquisition. In requital of this service, if he should be inclined to render it to them, they offered no less a sum than 800,000 crowns of gold. Charles received them favourably, and his council advised the acceptance of their offer. But Cardinal Ximenes, who had succeeded Torquemada as Inquisitor General, interfered, and sternly warned Charles that he could not comply with the request without unfaithfulness to Christ. Charles yielded, as his grandfather had yielded to Torquemada, and the petition of the Jews was rejected. Under the same influence he refused the Portuguese refugees permission to continue in Holland, whither many of them had fled. All who had not resided for six years in that country were obliged to quit it.

In 1521 John III. succeeded Emmanuel as King of Portugal. The latter had promised the New Christians, on their consenting to receive baptism, that the Inquisition should not be introduced into Portugal.[169] But some of John's advisers persuaded him that this promise was not binding, for two reasons—first, because the New Christians were notoriously unfaithful to their engagements; and secondly, because he had no power to make such an agreement without the consent of the Pope. To the Pope therefore John appealed for leave to set up the Holy Tribunal. But Clement VII. and his cardinals at once refused the petition, and ordered that all the New Christians whom John had arrested should be set at liberty. When, in 1534, Paul III. succeeded Clement, John renewed his petition. But Paul rejected it as resolutely as his predecessor had done, pointing out that Emmanuel's promises ought in honour and good faith to be respected.

John, however, was not to be discouraged. Learning that the Emperor Charles V. was on his way homeward, after his military success at Tunis, he resolved to avail himself of the opportunity. Charles would be entitled by the exploits he had performed to a triumph, at which custom allowed him to ask any favour he pleased from the Pope. He besought Charles therefore to make the establishment of the Inquisition in Portugal the privileged request. Charles assented,[170] and the Pope, though sorely unwilling, was obliged to grant it. At the same time, however, he stipulated that all the Portuguese Jews who had been imprisoned up to that time should be released from prison, and receive a free pardon. This condition the king refused to comply with; and the Pope had to exercise his personal authority, placarding the pardons on the doors of the churches, and sending his own officers to release the prisoners. The Inquisition, however, was set up in Portugal; and the same results attended the measure as had followed from it elsewhere, on all other occasions. Many of the secret Jews, foreseeing these, fled to other lands; where, if not actually safe from persecution, they would be at all events less liable to it.

Not many years afterwards, Jews and New Christians were to be met with in considerable numbers in various parts of the newly discovered regions of America, both in the countries which had been taken possession of by Spain and those which had fallen to the share of Portugal. In Africa also, and all over Asia, they settled—sometimes a scattered few, sometimes in larger communities. So numerous, indeed, were the emigrants, and so injurious to the national welfare was their departure found to be, that repeated edicts were issued by the kings of Portugal, forbidding it on the severest penalties. The simple method of detaining them, by making their residence in the country agreeable, or even endurable, to them, does not seem to have been thought of.

In Europe their chief place of retreat was Holland. While this was under the government of Spain, they were as sternly excluded from it as from every other portion of his Catholic Majesty's dominions. But when the long struggle for independence ended in the emancipation of the Seven United Provinces, the Spanish and Portuguese emigrants were favourably received there. In 1590, three Portuguese Jews, the advanced guard, so to speak, of a numerous host which was to follow, were hospitably entertained. From Embden in 1594 came ten more, who had borne the Portuguese names of Lopes Homen and Pereira, but who, as soon as they had settled in the Dutch capital, resumed their original designation of Abendana. The first synagogue was built there, in 1598. Notwithstanding the flight, however, of so many of the so-called New Christians from Portugal, enough of them remained behind to form a powerful party in the capital, which more than once, during the latter part of the century, interfered with considerable effect in the affairs of the State.

It remains that we say somewhat more respecting those Jews who still continued, as we have said, to reside in Spain and Portugal. A stranger, and at the same time a more instructive, history is not to be found in the annals of the world. Bigotry has never been so blind, so determined, so unscrupulous, as it was in Spain under the iron rule of the Inquisition. Arbitrary power has never been exercised more freely, more persistently, more pitilessly, than by Torquemada and his successors. The eyes of the Inquisition were everywhere—spying out men's ways, not only in their discharge of public duties, but following them, Argus-like, into the privacy of their family intercourse—nay, into the solitude of their closets and bedchambers. Their ears drank in men's secret whispers, uttered only in the hearing of their nearest intimates—their wives or their children. They did not hesitate to inflict the most dreadful tortures in order to elicit the information they desired. They spared, in the prosecution of their task, neither the weakness of womanhood, the tenderness of infancy, nor the infirmities of age. Yet they could not penetrate the mystery of secret Judaism. Men obtained the highest rank in the State, and filled the most important offices, honoured and dreaded by all men, who nevertheless belonged to this despised and proscribed race. The blood which was supposed so to degrade the man in whose veins it ran was owned by the greatest and noblest of the land—the marquis, the duke, and the prince, with their high-sounding titles and their lengthy pedigrees. Towards the end of the eighteenth century, it is related of the celebrated Portuguese minister, Pombal, that the king, having proposed at a meeting of the council that all who were of Jewish descent should be obliged thenceforth to appear in yellow caps, attended at the next council with three yellow caps in his hand. The king having inquired the meaning of this procedure, he replied that it was intended to carry out the proposition the king had made. 'One cap,' he observed, 'is for your majesty, one for the Grand Inquisitor, and the third for myself.'

Stranger still, but equally certain, is the fact that secret Jews held posts of dignity, not in the State only, but the Church also. There were convents full of Jewish monks and Jewish nuns. Priests said mass at the altars, and received confessions, and pronounced absolution, who regarded all these rites as false and impious. Nay, secret Jews wielded the powers of the Holy Office itself. They saw men dragged before them, and tortured and condemned them to the stake, for holding precisely the same faith as themselves—pronounced, it may be, the sentence with their own lips, and then went to their homes to take part in the proscribed rites themselves. If anything could prove more clearly than has been already proved, the folly, no less than wickedness, of religious persecution, it would surely be this strange and startling history.[171]

Nor ought we to quit this subject without remarking on the just and stern retribution with which the nation has been visited that did these things. At the beginning of the sixteenth century Spain was the leading power in Europe, containing forty millions of inhabitants, for which its rich and productive soil afforded ample subsistence. The empire of the New World, which was, as it were, committed to her care, poured wealth without limit into her lap. What is she now? Abroad, her name carries little respect; she has sunk to a secondary rank among the nations. Her voice is never heard in the settlement of European interests. At home, her population has diminished to little more than one-third of what it was four centuries before; her commerce is paralysed; her government unsettled. The poverty and ignorance of her people seem to be ever on the increase, and strife and anarchy continually distract the land. Who can doubt that her double sin— against the Indians of the New World, and the Jews of the Old—has brought down this heavy judgment on her?

FOOTNOTES:

[169] In the account given at the time of their conversion (1497), it is said that the Inquisition was not to be introduced 'for twenty years,' viz., till 1517. But it is plain that there must have been another promise for a longer period, though

no record has been preserved of it. The Pope, indeed, Paul III., plainly said as much.

[170] Charles, throughout his reign, was harsh and stern in his dealings with the Jews. His private secretary, Solomon Maleho, who had been an enforced convert to Christianity, afterwards returned to his old belief, and tried to convert the Emperor to it. The latter handed him over to the secular arm at Mantua, and he was burned at the stake.

[171] For a vivid picture of the strange condition of society in Spain at this period, the reader should study Miss Grace D'Aguilar's beautiful little tale, entitled *The Vale of Cedars*. See also some striking details in Borrow's *Bible in Spain*.

CHAPTER XXXI
A.D. 1500-1600. THE JEWS IN GERMANY AND CENTRAL EUROPE

The condition of the Jews during the sixteenth century in those parts of Germany and Central Europe where their presence was still tolerated, does not materially differ from what it had been for many previous generations. We hear of fewer outbreaks of lawless violence, and the atrocities committed on them seem a shade less barbarous. But the history is in the main such as the Christian chronicler must record, and the Christian reader peruse, with feelings of shame and sorrow. At Mecklenberg, just at the end of the previous century, the oft-repeated, though never proved, accusation had been revived of bribing a Christian priest to sell the consecrated Host; which the Jews who purchased it immediately proceeded to stab, drawing forth (it was alleged) the very blood of the Lord Jesus, whose body it was. A grave and minute inquiry was set on foot. Thirty Jews, together with the priest, were condemned to be burned at the stake for the offence. Some Jewish women and children were implicated in the charge. One of the former is related to have put two of her daughters to death, in order to save them from the horrors that awaited them, and to have been on the point of killing a third, when she was snatched from her. Two years afterwards, another charge was brought against some Hungarian Jews, or rather another form of the same charge: this time the offence being murdering a Christian in order to drink his blood.[172] The accused were put to the torture—not so much, we learn, to elicit the fact whether *they* were guilty, as whether the whole Jewish people of Hungary were not implicated in the crime. Monstrous as this may seem, it was not the first time, by any means, that such a belief had been entertained.[173] Possibly, indeed, it was hoped that under the pressure of their agony the sufferers would confess that, or anything else that they were required to admit, and so give a pretext for a general massacre. If so, the attempt failed, for we find that only those who had been accused of the crime suffered for it.

A few years afterwards, at Nuremberg, and again at Cologne, expulsions of the Jews took place. In both cities, though a number of charges were alleged against them, the real offence seems to have been their commercial success, and the heavy load of debt contracted to them by the citizens of the two towns. The shortest mode of paying off the liabilities, it was found, lay in finding their creditors guilty of some offence for which they were punishable by the confiscation of their property, including, of course, all debts owing to them. But these expulsions, however unjust, do not appear to have been stained by the additional guilt of bloodshed.

In 1509, a Jew who had been converted to Christianity, Pfeffercorn by name, filled with the zeal for which proselytes are always remarkable, suggested to the Emperor Maximilian that all books which upheld or set forth Jewish doctrine, and especially the Talmud, the great repository of Jewish fable, should be everywhere destroyed. He had already written more than one book, in which he charged his countrymen not only with denying the truth of the New Testament, but with departing from the commandments of the Old. He accused them also of using imprecations against Christians, both in public and private. These had so much effect upon Maximilian, that he is reported to have been half inclined to grant his request. He resolved, however, to appoint a commission of learned men to examine and report on the matter. At the head of this was placed Reuchlin[174] (otherwise Capnio), the most famous Hebrew scholar of his day, and a man of large and liberal views. He advised the Emperor that such of the Jewish books as contained blasphemies against our Lord (as undoubtedly some of them did) had better be destroyed; but those which simply treated of the tenets and ritual of the Jews ought to be retained. He pointed out how impossible it was to suppress books which a certain number of readers were resolved to preserve. This would have been at any time difficult, but since the invention of printing it had become morally impossible, as the Jews had now begun to make free use of the printing-press.[175] We cannot wonder much that a man of Pfeffercorn's temper would not acquiesce in a decision like this. He attacked Reuchlin in an angry pamphlet, to which Reuchlin replied. The dispute was referred to the Pope, and Hochstraten, a Dutch Inquisitor who had espoused Pfeffercorn's quarrel, repaired to Rome to advocate it; but the papal decision was in favour of Reuchlin. The Jewish books were spared. Nevertheless, it may be doubted whether the affair was favourable to them. The result was to attract the attention of Christian scholars to these Jewish attacks on Christianity, and replies were in consequence written, which were probably more damaging to Judaism than any burning of their books could have been.

Out of this controversy a number of sects seem to have arisen—at least, they are first noticed by writers about this time, and they disappear from history soon afterwards. Among these Seidelius of Silesia, George de Novara, and Francis David are the most remarkable.[176] They held opinions culled, some from Judaism, some from Christianity, and differed widely from one another. They had the usual fate of eclectics, being rejected and despised by both parties.

In 1516 the Jews had a narrow escape of being expelled from Frankfort. An assembly, consisting of deputies from various sovereigns and free towns, was held in that city, for the purpose of organizing measures for their banishment. Fortunately for them, the deputies could not agree among themselves. The Jews were, however, driven out of Brandenburg. Lippold, physician to the elector of that country, was charged with having poisoned his employer. He made a confession under torture, and was executed; after which all his countrymen were driven into exile.

Towards the middle of this century the Jews were for the first time expelled from Prague. They had dwelt unmolested in that city from time immemorial. No one knew when they had first settled there; but tradition said it was in times when Bohemia was yet heathen; and inscriptions on some of the older graves in their moss-grown cemetery are quoted in proof of the fact. The very latest date assigned for their arrival is the tenth century of Christianity. They had built a noble synagogue, and had opened an academy, over which a renowned Jewish doctor presided. But in the troubled times which followed the burning of Huss and Jerome of Prague they continually fell under the suspicion of one, or, it might be said, both parties, the Jews being too cautious to ally themselves with either. This feeling grew stronger when the Reformation itself had fairly engaged men's minds. Among the mutual jealousies and suspicions which had taken possession of men's minds, that of the secret plottings of the Jews in favour of their antagonists, was one of constant occurrence. It chanced that terrible conflagrations broke out in some of the larger cities, and among others, in Prague. The Jews were instantly suspected of having caused it. Being suspected was in those times very nearly the same thing as being convicted of it. All those that escaped the flames were banished from the city, with the exception of ten families, who obtained permission to remain. The Emperor was not convinced of their guilt, but the feeling that had been provoked was too strong for him to cope with. He saw plainly that nothing but the death or the banishment of Jews would satisfy the people, and he chose the more merciful of the alternatives offered him. Towards the latter end of the year the real incendiaries were discovered, and the Jews were then permitted to return.

About eight years afterwards another outcry was raised, this time it being affirmed that the Jews had been praying that disaster and ruin might befall the Christians. Their books were seized as a punishment, and carried off to Vienna, so that the Rabbins had to officiate in the synagogues as well as they were able, reciting everything from memory. We must suppose that this charge was disproved, as the other had been, for the books were soon afterwards restored. Even this was not the end of their troubles. Before the year was out, there came another peremptory order for all the Jews, except the ten privileged families, once more to leave the city and settle elsewhere in Bohemia; and this time it does not appear that they were allowed to return.

Merseburg again—the capital now of one of the regencies of the Prussian States, which consists almost entirely of cessions made by Saxony in 1815—was another of the cities in which the Jews claimed to have resided without interruption for nearly fourteen centuries. Yet, so widespread had the feeling against them become, that they were forced, in 1559, to quit this city also, notwithstanding that the Emperor Ferdinand was willing to help them to the utmost of his ability. He not only protected them, indeed, but granted them a privilege which had been accorded to their ancestors in the East, many centuries before—that of having their own special ruler, who was known by the same title as that borne in the earliest Christian times by the Patriarch of the East, viz., the 'Prince of the Captivity.'

In Moravia, in 1574, a similar flame of persecution broke out. We are not informed what were the precise charges, but no doubt they were much the same that were alleged against almost all Jewish congregations in Central Europe about this time. Many Jews, we learn, were burnt at the stake, and many more put to death in other ways. They appealed to the Emperor Ferdinand, who appears always to have been willing to assist his Jewish subjects to the best of his ability. He did interfere, and stopped the executions, but not before many victims had been sacrificed.

In Franconia, six years afterwards, there was something of a similar outbreak. In this instance the Jews were accused, as they were in many other places, of having set on fire the town of Bamberg. But here they escaped without undergoing any further severity than having to make good the loss which those had suffered whose property had been destroyed.

In Poland and the Ukraine a more merciful state of things prevailed. In both these the Jews enjoyed entire freedom alike from pillage and persecution. In the first-named country they were chiefly engaged in trade, which they almost monopolized; in the latter, almost exclusively in agriculture.

But in Russia proper the race of Israel continued to be, as tradition declares it always to have been, harshly treated—such Israelites, that is to say, as were still permitted to dwell in the country, the Jews generally having been expelled from it, as the reader has learned (a.d. 1113). Late, however, in the previous, and early in the present century, during the last years of the long reign of Ivan III., a most singular apostasy to Judaism is recorded to have taken place, the truth of which we should certainly be inclined to doubt, if it had not been so respectably attested. A Jew named Zacharias, about a.d. 1490, began to attempt the conversion of certain Russian priests to Judaism, and succeeded to an extraordinary extent in the design. The converts adopted all the Jewish rites, except that of circumcision; which they dispensed with, because, in event of discovery, it would be a certain proof against them. The apostasy spread rapidly and widely. Ecclesiastics occupying the highest positions in the Church, even the Patriarch Zosimus himself, became perverts. The conspiracy, if it may be so called, was at last discovered, and a great number of these 'secret Jews' summoned before the council and convicted. They were punished after a more merciful manner than that adopted towards their brethren in Spain. They were set on horseback, with their faces towards the tails of their steeds, dressed after a bizarre fashion to resemble devils, and paraded through the streets amid the jeers of the rabble. Zosimus was sent back to the monastery of which he had been archimandrite. But, though the evil was detected, it is doubtful whether it was extirpated. It is said to have lingered in the Russian Church long afterwards.

Rabbi Joseph ben Meir is the great Jewish historian of this period. He was born at Avignon in 1496, and wrote a *Universal History,* and a *History of his own Times.* The latter, though its statements must be taken with reserve, is regarded generally as a valuable book. David Gans also, born 1541, was a renowned scholar and author. He died in Prague, a.d. 1613.

FOOTNOTES:

[172] See Appendix V.

[173] In the reign of Henry III. in England, at the inquest held on Hugh of Lincoln, a.d. 1255, it was declared that the whole of the Jews in England were privy to, and guilty of, the crime.

[174] Johann Reuchlin was born at Pforzheim, December 28, 1455, of poor parents. The sweetness of his voice attracted attention to him, and he was sent to be educated at Paris. He began his career as a teacher of classics at Basle, but soon abandoned this for the profession of the law. In 1482 he had become known as a Hebrew scholar, and he was noticed by the Emperor Frederick III. In 1498 he returned to Stuttgard, where his fame continued to increase; in consequence

of which Pfeffercorn's proposals were submitted to him by Maximilian. The most celebrated satire of the day, the *Epistola Obscurorum Virorum*, was written to uphold his views, and had the effect of completely crushing his adversaries. Reuchlin died at Stuttgard, December, 1521.

[175] Some of the Jewish books were no doubt extremely offensive to Christians, as, for example, the *Chisuk Emunah* of Isaac ben Abraham, a Polish Jew. The Portuguese Jews translated it into their own language, and diffused it widely. The *Nitzachon* again, ascribed to Rabbi Lipman, of Mulhouse, was equally, if not more virulent. It could hardly be expected that even the wisest and most far-seeing men of the sixteenth century would tolerate these.

[176] Seidelius taught that Messiah, when He came, would come to the Jews only, the Gentiles having neither part nor lot in Him. Francis David acknowledged Jesus Christ, but held that it was sinful to pray to Him. George de Novara claimed to believe Christian doctrine, but denied that Messiah had come. He was burnt at the stake.

CHAPTER XXXII
A.D. 1500-1600. THE JEWS
IN ASIA AND AFRICA

We have now recorded the fortunes of the Jews, during the sixteenth century, in all the countries of Europe where a domicile was allowed them, as well as in Spain and Portugal, where, though banished by law, they were still, under a nominal profession of Christianity, permitted to linger. We have now once again to transfer our attention to eastern and southern lands, in which, under Mahometan rule, they found a more merciful refuge. Before doing so, however, it is proper to repeat the remark already made, that, although legally forbidden, during those centuries, to enter several of the European kingdoms, it is far from certain that they were not to be found in them, and that in no inconsiderable numbers, though doubtless they were careful to keep out of sight as much as possible. Reference has been made to a Spanish historian, who says that 'many of the Spanish exiles fled to England, establishing themselves in three of the largest towns—Dover, York, and London—and that they built synagogues in the last-named city, where they afterwards carried on a thriving trade.' 'From 1291 to 1655,' writes a pamphleteer in 1753, 'the Jews have run the hazard, as they do in another country [doubtless Spain], where so many of them have expired, and annually still expire in the flames; but meeting all along with lenitives [merciful usage], they have made true one of our English proverbs of claiming an ell's longitude for an inch's allowance.'[177]

In France it is certain that they were tolerated, so long, probably, as they did not make themselves conspicuous. Rabbi Joseph relates that Henry II. allowed certain Jews from Mauritius to reside in the French cities, and in 1550 granted them his protection and various privileges. His father and his queen, Catherine de Medici, had Jewish physicians, who were high in favour with their employers. We are told that the Parliament of Paris condemned in severe terms the inhuman conduct of the sovereigns of Spain and Portugal; and that many of the Portuguese emigrants were suffered to establish themselves at Bordeaux and Bayonne, where they have since resided without molestation. The same, no doubt, was the case among the German States; where, if the Jews were persecuted in one city, it was comparatively easy to fly for shelter to another.

So likewise in Russia. The Jews have never been readmitted to the provinces from which they were originally driven out. But Russia has in modern times acquired by conquest extensive territories in which there was a large Hebrew population. She did not carry her dislike so far as to expel them from her new dominions, and has as many as two millions of Jewish subjects. But her feelings towards them have undergone but little change.

Doubtless many of the Spanish and Portuguese fugitives betook themselves to one or other of the above-named countries. But it is tolerably certain that the great mass chose the Mussulman kingdoms in Asia and Africa as their future abiding-places. Whether it was due to the scorn, the calm indifference, or the compassion, with which the Mahometan princes regarded them, it is certain that they permitted them the free exercise of their religion, and the full possession of civil rights. In Persia and Media, even before the Spanish exodus, they seem to have been very numerous, though the particulars recorded respecting them are extremely scanty. During Timour's wars, they naturally suffered, among all the other inhabitants of Persia, from the inroads of his savage soldiery, which took little account of the difference of creed among those whom they attacked and conquered. We are informed that their synagogues were wrecked, their schools destroyed, and great numbers of them slain in the capture of cities. These troubles had hardly subsided when the irruption of the fierce Shah Ismail Sofi once more threw everything into disorder. His rapid and signal success is said to have produced such an effect upon them, that they were persuaded he must be the Messiah who was to come. The idea was encouraged by the fact that Ismail had declared himself to be a prophet sent from God to reform the corruptions of Islamism. But he received their homage very coldly[178]— indeed, is said to have treated them with less consideration than any others of his new subjects.

One of his successors, Shah Abbas, a generation or two afterwards, brought about a severe persecution of the Jews in his dominions, though in a very singular manner. He had issued a proclamation granting great privileges to such strangers as should settle in his dominions. The Jews immediately availed themselves of this, and crowded in such numbers into the country that they speedily engrossed the trade. This was no more than was their ordinary wont; but Shah Abbas's subjects were greatly aggrieved, and made bitter complaints to the king. Thereupon he made a very minute inquiry into their peculiar habits and opinions, possibly in order to find some excuse for banishing them from the land. Learning that they had long expected the arrival of their Messiah, and were still waiting for Him, he insisted on it that they should name some time by which, if He had not made His appearance, they should admit their belief to be unfounded, and conform to Mahometanism. After long consultation among themselves, they told Shah Abbas that they would agree to fix seventy years as the prescribed limit—doubtless arguing that most probably all concerned, but certainly Shah Abbas, would be dead before the arrival of that day. The king received the reply with gravity, and caused it to be formally registered, and deposited in the archives of the kingdom. It is probable that the memory of it died out even before the end of Shah Abbas's reign. At all events, when the appointed period approached, wars and commotions of one kind or another occupied men's minds, and no attention was paid to the subject. But, more than a hundred years afterwards, Shah Abbas II., in an unlucky hour, chanced to light upon his ancestor's decree. It was of course found that, although the seventy years had long expired, and the expected Messiah had not made His appearance, the Jews had not adopted the Moslem faith, nor were they disposed to do so now. Here was a clear proof of their treachery and falsehood; and the consequence was a massacre which is said to have lasted for three years, those only escaping who abjured their religion, or fled into Turkey on one side, or India on the other. After a while, however, it was found that the supposed converts, though nominally Mahometans, as their brethren in Spain had professed to be Christians, were in reality Jews at heart. Wiser than Ferdinand and his successors, Shah Abbas recalled his decree, and allowed the pretended Mussulmans to return to their real creed.

But little is known of the Jews in the Eastern Empire during the period preceding the capture of Constantinople by the Turks, in 1453. But, a generation or two after that event, large numbers were to be found both in Constantinople itself and other parts of the Sultan's European dominions. The Spanish exiles who resorted thither found a large number of synagogues already in existence, served by a priesthood in no way inferior to what their own had been at home. They did not, however, amalgamate with these, but built new synagogues in Constantinople, Jerusalem, Damascus, Saloniki, and other great cities, each of which long afterwards retained the name of the original builders, one being called the synagogue of Toledo, another of Lisbon, another of Aragon, and the like. The Turkish government treated them with great liberality, allowing them unrestricted freedom in establishing manufactures and transacting commerce, permitting them also to hold landed property. Whatever amount of their wealth had been stripped from them by their Spanish persecutors, we may be sure, was now speedily recovered. Nor does it appear that they were subjected to any excessive exactions. They paid a certain amount of taxes, no doubt, and were occasionally liable to arbitrary demands, from which no one in the East is secure; but, on the whole, they were mercifully dealt with. Here too, as in all other lands where they have resided, their great financial and diplomatic ability was utilized by the Turkish rulers. Selim I. (a.d. 1512) trusted much to his Jewish physician, Joseph Hamon. His son, Solyman II., called 'the Magnificent' (a.d. 1520), similarly employed Moses Hamon, the son of Joseph, who, by his influence with his royal master, on one occasion saved the whole of his people from massacre.[179] Solomon Ashkenasi was selected as the Sultan's agent to conduct a negotiation with the Venetian Republic. Joseph Nasi obtained such favour with Selim II. (a.d. 1566) that he was made Duke of Naxos, and was even designated King of Cyprus, though that intention was never carried out. After the disastrous battle of Lepanto, another Jew, Solomon Rophé, was sent to arrange a treaty of peace with the Venetians.

The Spanish Jews, among their other effects, brought their printing-presses into Turkey, where, by the favour of the Sultans, they were set up. At Constantinople and at Saloniki they were soon in active employment. The Old Testament Scriptures in Hebrew and Spanish were printed and largely circulated, as well as many Jewish writings which had hitherto remained in manuscript. At Saloniki a famous college was established, at which there were said to be as many as 5000 students. There was also a valuable library, which unfortunately was destroyed by fire in 1545.

The Holy Land is another country to which, as we might naturally expect, refugees from other lands resorted. It had always been regarded as a befitting thing for Jews of an advanced age to make a pilgrimage thither, and die among the hallowed scenes of their cherished traditions. With every persecution in European countries the number of these increased; and at the beginning of the sixteenth century Palestine was filled with swarms of Israelites, who, as a rule, were poor and destitute, and suffered greatly from the rapacity of Turkish officials. The Jewish communities in other parts of the world regarded it as their duty to support these needy brethren, and in larger cities collections were regularly made in the synagogues for this purpose. As no attempt apparently was made to provide them with the means of supporting themselves,—and possibly none could have been made with success,—the distress was always considerable, and after the Spanish exodus rose to a still greater height.

Another quarter to which large numbers of the expelled Jews migrated was the northern coast of Africa. This was a region already familiar to them. Egypt had, for a great length of time, been a favourite place of abode with them, and this had more particularly been the case since the time of Maimonides. Schools had been established in Cairo, Damietta, and other Egyptian towns, to which great numbers of students resorted. In the kingdom of Morocco, again, the banished Jews settled in great numbers. This was, indeed, the nearest country to Spain, Portugal excepted, and communications had for a long time been kept up between the inhabitants of the two kingdoms. In Tripoli also, Oran, Fez, Tunis, and Algiers, many Jewish families established themselves. But they did not receive the same friendly welcome which their brethren experienced in the East. They were allowed liberty of conscience, no doubt, and the protection of the law; but that was all the favour accorded them. The authorities laid heavy burdens on them, and at times exacted large sums as subsidies, after a fashion which greatly resembled the dealings of the English and French sovereigns several centuries before. The lower orders looked on them with fanatical prejudice, and they were obliged to wear black turbans, and boots of a different colour from those of the natives of the country. Yet their position, on the whole, was not unhappy. They were largely employed in the iron-works among the mountains of Morocco, as well as in building and agriculture.

One feature in their history deserves especial mention. In 1578, when the ill-fated expedition of Sebastian of Portugal took place, large numbers of Portuguese nobles and gentlemen were made prisoners, and sold as slaves in the market-places of the chief towns of Morocco. Many of these were bought by Portuguese Jews, who must have been sorely tempted to requite the injuries themselves and their fathers had received on these captives, who were wholly at their mercy. But they took a nobler revenge. They not only exacted no ransom of them, but allowed them to return to their homes, requiring of them no other condition than that of passing their word of honour that they would, on arriving in Portugal, remit to their former masters the sums that had been paid for their redemption from slavery. History has recorded few nobler actions.

FOOTNOTES:

[177] *Some Observations of a London Merchant about the Bill for the Naturalization of the Jews*, a.d. 1753. The writer had probably conversed with persons who remembered the state of things in England before the readmission of the Jews. As regards the assertion of the Spanish historian, therefore, there is very reasonable likelihood of the Jews having been allowed to live without molestation in England during the reigns of the Tudors. Indeed, as Disraeli has remarked, if there had been no Jews in England, Sir E. Coke would hardly have insisted so forcibly on their not being admissible as witnesses. But the statement respecting the building and

public use of synagogues must be taken with reservation. The expulsion from Spain occurred a little before the close of the fifteenth century. Scarcely more than fifty years afterwards we find Cromwell's divines declaring that 'for the Jews to have synagogues, or any public meetings for worship, was not only evil, but scandalous to Christian churches.' Surely they could not have said this, if synagogues had so recently existed in London, and worship been celebrated in them!

[178] This king seems to have had a dislike to excessive homage, which was a rare feature in an Eastern prince. It is recorded of him that on one occasion, after one of his great victories, his soldiers saluted him with Oriental adulation, some declaring him to be a prophet, others an angel, and others God Himself. Finding that he could not dissuade them from their impiety, he ordered a deep pit to be dug, and then, throwing one of his shoes into it, gave out that the man who honoured him most was to fetch it out. Numbers instantly threw themselves into the pit. He then gave orders to have the earth thrown back again, burying the whole of his worshippers alive! Doubtless none ever offered him adoration again.

[179] A Turk, having reason to suspect one of his neighbours of an attempt to seduce his wife, assassinated him, and to escape suspicion threw the corpse into the Jewish quarter. It was found there, and occasioned a popular insurrection, in which the Jews would have been murdered to a man, if Moses Hamon had not prevailed on Solyman to order an inquiry, by which the truth was elicited.

CHAPTER XXXIII
A.D. 1600-1700. THE JEWS IN
GERMANY AND CENTRAL EUROPE

At the commencement of the seventeenth century the Reformation may be regarded as an accomplished fact. The great flood of controversy which had broken up the Church had begun to subside, and whatever countries had been gained by the new opinions, or had been retained by the old ones, remained in both instances firm to their allegiance. It might have been expected that the great changes which had been worked would largely affect the condition of the Jews, and ultimately, no doubt, they did so; but for the time the effects were scarcely discernible. No doubt, in Protestant countries the clergy could no longer put in force the terrible engines of persecution which had hitherto been ready to their hand; and this was in itself an immense relief. Again, in lands which still owned the supremacy of Rome, much of the virulence of the priesthood against the Jews was of necessity abated. They had graver and more absorbing occupation for their thoughts. In the momentous struggle which was in progress the Jews were more or less overlooked. But the bitterness of feeling towards them was scarcely, if at all, diminished. The leaders of the Reformed movement themselves regarded the Jews with but little favour. They could not, indeed, but abhor the barbarities which had been employed against them by the rulers of the Church; but they had little idea, so far as themselves were concerned, of showing consideration towards the obstinate and rebellious race which persisted in rejecting Christ.[180] This, however, was not universally the case. Frank du Jon (Franciscus Junius), the well-known Dutch Reformer, urged on his countrymen, in earnest and emphatic language, the duty owing by all Christian nations to their brethren the Jews, who were to be won by the spirit of love to the fold of Christ. So did Isaac Vossius, Professor at Amsterdam, who addressed a letter to the Jews, strongly indicative of this temper. The Arminians of Holland again, and their allies, evinced a most brotherly kindness towards such Jews as had taken refuge in their country. The celebrated Hugo Grotius was especially remarkable for the respect he entertained for the Rabbins and their opinions. Indeed, though some of the leading Reformers occasionally expressed themselves in a manner which was inconsistent with the wise principles they professed, yet the general effect of their teaching grew and strengthened as generations went on, and resulted at last in a widespread and enlightened toleration.

It must also be remembered that the Jews themselves—for a long time, at all events—showed no more inclination to embrace Gospel truth, as set forth by the Reformers, than they had been in previous generations to accept the tenets of the Romish Church. It was not, indeed, to be expected that the deep mutual rancour which had been the growth of so many generations— of savage cruelty on the one hand, and sullen, inflexible hate on the other, could be removed by any sudden change, even if its results had been far more beneficent. It is far easier to provoke international animosities than to compose them again. Let us remember how long, in this country, the bitter dislike and contempt of the French nation, which Nelson and his school did their best to encourage as the best safeguard of England against successful invasion—let us remember, I say, how long it lasted, after all possible danger of the dreaded results had passed away. It cannot, indeed, be said to be dead even now, though three generations have passed away since it was called forth. Remember also that the mutual antipathy of the Englishman and the Frenchman could not for a moment be compared, in respect of its bitterness, with that which existed in those dark and miserable times between the Jew and the Christian. Let us be thankful that a spirit of toleration and mercy has been growing, however slowly, and still continues to grow, and pray that our children may behold the ripe perfection of that glorious harvest.

Not much is recorded of the Jews in Germany and the other countries of Central Europe during the earlier portion of the seventeenth century. There was a disturbance at Frankfort in 1614, which proved disastrous to them, though it does not seem to have arisen from religious bitterness. It will be remembered that, as nearly as possible one hundred years before, there had been a proposal to exile all the Jews in the town. That originated in commercial animosity, and nothing but the mutual jealousies of the deputies present at the meeting had prevented its being carried out. On the present occasion a revolt of the trade guilds against the town authorities had been successful, and the first act of the guilds was to expel the Hebrew traders, of whose prosperity they were jealous. But two years afterwards the sedition was suppressed, and the leader of the *émeute* put to death, whereupon the Jews were permitted to return. A similar expulsion took place in Worms, when the fugitives found a protector in the Elector Frederick.

In the year 1619 began the terrible 'Thirty Years' War,' from which all classes of men suffered heavily, and the Jews as much as any. During the celebrated siege of Prague they rendered great service to the Emperor.

Rabbi Leo has written a history of the incidents of that eventful period; in which he praises highly the conduct of his countrymen, their zeal and courage throughout the siege, and especially their piety, in assembling in their synagogues to implore Heaven to grant their countrymen victory, and reciting a litany composed expressly for the occasion by one of their Rabbins. He is persuaded, indeed, that the preservation of the city was entirely owing to their intercession.

If such was the case, it is to be feared that the Emperors Ferdinand II. and III. did not evince the gratitude which would be due from them. We learn that in 1630 the first-named took from them their privilege of farming the revenues of the Hungarian kingdom. His reason for doing so does not flatter them. He says it was because 'they had neither conscience nor honesty, and were therefore unworthy to enjoy it.' They must, however, have regained it, since we find that they were again deprived of it, in 1647, by his successors.

In 1650 a great meeting of Jews, at which three hundred Rabbins were present, is said to have been held on the plain of Ageda, thirty miles from Buda, to determine a question which, it appeared, was agitating the minds of many—whether the Messiah had not already come. The sole authority for the occurrence appears to be one Samuel Brett, who published an account of it in London, a.d. 1655, five years after the supposed assembly. Most historians reject the story as a mere invention, designed partly to facilitate the conversion of the Jews, partly to throw obloquy on the Church of Rome. Among those who refuse it credit, is the celebrated Menasseh ben Israel, whose authority carries great weight. Further, in the narrative itself, the imputing by the Pharisees of the miracles of our Lord to the agency of magic, reads like a plagiarism from Matt. xii. 24; as also their objections to His mean origin, to a similar extract from Mark vi. 3.[181]

On the other hand, some authorities accept Brett's statement as genuine; and there are circumstances in it not easy to reconcile with the notion of imposture. Thus, the author gives his name and the particulars of his own life and career, which it would have been easy to disprove, if they were fictitious; and, as the publication of the story must have provoked a good deal of angry feeling, it is at least strange that this was not done. But when Nathaniel Holmes republished the history, as he did eleven years afterwards, he added no hint that its authenticity had been so much as suspected. Nor again, still later, did the compiler of the *Harleian Miscellany*, who also reproduced it. Further, Brett states that the Jews, when they broke up their meeting, resolved to hold another in three years from that time— two years, that is, after the date of Brett's publication. An impostor, one would think, would not have inserted this perfectly needless addition to his narrative, which could only lead to his detection. The idea which the entire story gives is rather exaggeration than imposture. Such a meeting as he describes might really have taken place; but the numbers, the character of the speakers, and the interest felt by the Jews generally in the proceedings, have been greatly overstated. It will be better to give Brett's story with this caution appended to it.

He states that the first meeting took place at the time and for the purpose already stated, the King of Hungary having first granted permission. A vast number of learned Jews from all nations repaired to the spot, and encamped in tents round a central pavilion, where the council sat.

The first day was employed in examining the credentials of the various Rabbins. On the second, Rabbi Zechariah, who had been chosen president, proposed the main question, 'Whether the Messiah had already come, or were they still to await His advent?' Some, we are told, argued that He must have come. They had now suffered, they said, for 1600 years the heaviest woes, nor did there seem any prospect of these coming to an end. But why should God thus delay the coming of the Deliverer? Neither they, nor their fathers for many generations, had been guilty of idolatry, which alone would be an adequate cause for withholding Him. But the sense of the assembly was against this view. It was affirmed that He had not come, and that the sins of the people had delayed His advent.

Next it was debated in what manner He would come; and here there was no lack of unanimity. It was agreed that He would appear, according to the old belief, as a conqueror, who would restore the kingdom to Israel; that He would uphold the Mosaic law in all its integrity, and that He would be born of a virgin. Some of those present then raised the question whether Jesus the crucified might not be the Messiah. But the Pharisees objected that Jesus had been a person of low birth and condition, whereas the Messiah would appear surrounded by all the accessories of earthly grandeur. A Rabbi named Abraham rejoined that it was difficult to account for the miracles wrought by Jesus, unless He was the Messiah. But Zebedee, a chief Pharisee, rejoined that these miracles had been effected by magic. In this the Sadducees present concurred, though they had hitherto opposed nearly all that the Pharisees advanced.

The congress had lasted for six days, when some priests made their appearance, who, at the request of the King of Hungary, had been despatched from Rome. These at first only attempted to prove that Jesus was the Messiah, and, while discoursing on this topic, seem to have been heard with patience. But when, digressing from this, they began to insist on the authority of the Church, and demand the submission of the Jews to the Pope, the whole assembly broke out into a tumultuous cry of 'No Christ!' 'No God-man!' 'No intercession of saints!' 'No worship of images!' 'No prayers to the Virgin!' The meeting broke up in disorder, coming to no conclusion. But it was alleged that many Jews were shaken in their belief.

In another part of Europe—the part, indeed, in which the Jews had hitherto enjoyed the most entire immunity from suffering—great troubles befell them about this time, in consequence of the rebellion of the Cossacks against the rule of the Poles. In the spring of 1648 massacres of Jews took place in the countries which lie to the east of the Dnieper, in which thousands perished. Still larger numbers were carried off as prisoners, and sold in Turkey. During the interregnum following on the death of King Ladislaus, hordes of barbarians overran the Ukraine, committing great havoc, from which all the inhabitants suffered, but none, we are told, so much as the Jews.

In 1670 the Jews were banished from the Austrian dominions by the Emperor Leopold, a weak and narrow-minded prince, who was easily persuaded to adopt measures which he was as speedily obliged to modify or reverse. He had granted, only a short time before, Rabbi Zachariah permission to build a magnificent synagogue and schools for the revival of learning. But the synagogue had hardly been finished when it was turned into a Christian church by the Emperor, and the whole of the Jews exiled from his dominions. The reason of this is said to have been that the Empress attributed her barrenness to the displeasure of Heaven at the toleration shown to the Jews. But her death in her confinement, shortly afterwards, doubtless had a counter-effect on the mind of the Emperor; and we are not surprised to hear that the Jews were recalled, and re-established in their possessions.[182] It was upon this occasion that the Jews expelled from Vienna found a refuge in Berlin, where a thriving community grew up.

In this century many learned Jews and Christian Hebrew scholars appeared, whose names are well known, even at the present day. Among these the most distinguished were Rabbi Menasseh, of whom we shall have occasion to speak presently, and the Christian writers Pocock, Surenhusius, and Vitringa. But the most renowned Christian Hebraists of this century were the two Buxtorfs. The elder, Johann, born at Westphalia in 1564, and dying in Basle in 1629, is the author of the famous Hebrew dictionary and grammar continually quoted by Hebrew scholars. His son, also called Johann, born 1599, and dying in 1664, finished the concordance which his father had commenced.

FOOTNOTES:

[180] It has already been observed that Martin Luther, though sometimes he speaks of the Jews rather with considerate compassion than anger, at other times, and especially later in his career, uses the very bitterest language respecting them, as, for instance, in his tract (published in 1543) on *The Jews and their Lies*, the title of which, it may be remarked, is quite in accordance with its contents. And again, in his exposition of Psalm xxii., written many years earlier, he thus writes: 'Doubt not, beloved in Christ, that after the devil, you have no more bitter, venomous, violent enemy than the Jew.' He also enjoins the sternest and most violent measures to be used against them. The great founder of Calvinism, again, though he is less fiery and vehement in his denunciation of them, cannot be said to regard them with any greater favour. He sees in them nothing but the virulent, determined enemies of Christ, whom it would be weakness, if not sin, to treat with any favour.

[181] It may be added that the very existence of the Sadducees, as a sect, at this period of history, is an anachronism.

[182] A different explanation has been given of Leopold's strange changes in his treatment of the Jews. He is said to have shown them favour at first, on account of his attachment to a beautiful Jewess. But she was assassinated; and Leopold, at first believing the deed to have been done by the Jews, banished them. Afterwards, being convinced of his mistake, he allowed them to return.

CHAPTER XXXIV
A.D. 1600-1700. THE JEWS IN HOLLAND.—DA COSTA, SPINOZA

The reader has already learned that, towards the close of the last century, many of the Portuguese exiles found a refuge from persecution in Holland. In truth, of all the countries of Europe, at this period of their history, none showed them such kindness as the republic of the Low Countries. If the Reformation had done the race of Israel no other service than that of opening to them this place of shelter, they would still have been largely indebted to it. No dream of the imagination could exceed the wretchedness of the Jews in Spain and Portugal at the outset of the seventeenth century. They had to choose between ruin, torture, and death on the one hand,—not for themselves only, but for their wives and children also,—or the surrender of their cherished faith, which was, in their eyes, the surrender of all hope, here and hereafter. Their only escape from these stern alternatives lay in a life-long duplicity and imposture, which must needs degrade them in their own eyes to the very dust. Of the three terrible issues thus offered them, we have seen that many of them did choose this last; but our contempt is disarmed, and only our pity is awakened, as we peruse their melancholy history. The toleration, however, that prevailed in Holland afforded a means of escape alike from the humiliation and the danger in which they were living. As the century advanced, increasing numbers of New Christians made their escape to the Low Countries, where they renounced the false profession they had made, and returned openly to their ancient worship. It has been already mentioned that in 1598 the first Jewish synagogue was built in Amsterdam. Ten or twelve years afterwards the numbers had so increased that a second became necessary, and in 1618 a third.

But it was not only the exiles from Spain and Portugal who crowded into Holland as a harbour of refuge. From many parts of Germany and the contiguous countries, whenever the flame of persecution broke out, as it was ever apt to do on the slightest provocation, the Jews, who had heard of the justice and favour shown to their countrymen by the Dutch, came to partake of it themselves. From Poland and Lithuania, again, thousands of Jews emigrated, driven from their homes by the ravages committed by the

Cossacks, who, under Chelmnicki, had risen against their Polish masters. A large proportion of these settled in the United Provinces. One company, which consisted of three thousand, landed at Texel, and there were many others almost as numerous. After some inquiry they were received at Amsterdam, and permission given them to build a synagogue.

Thus the Jews of Holland were divided into two societies which might be called the Spanish and the German synagogues.[183] Their religious tenets were doubtless in complete harmony. But they had different usages and historical traditions, and they are said to have entertained mutual jealousies and enmities. Possibly the imposture of Rabbi Zeigler, one of the numberless adventurers who have claimed to be the Messiah, or His forerunner, may have done something to create this severance. Zeigler professed to have seen the promised deliverer at Strasburg, and assured his countrymen that, as soon as they had declared their readiness to accept him, he would appear, destroy the kingdom of Christ (as he called the supremacy of the Gentiles), and extend his own from one end of the world to the other. The Messiah was also to hold a council at Constance, which would last for twelve years, and all religious difficulties would be composed at it. As the Messiah did not appear, Zeigler's followers were so far undeceived; but the mischief which his imposture had occasioned lasted long afterwards.

This epoch is remarkable for a demonstration of intolerant bigotry—not, as heretofore, evinced by the Christians against the Jews, but by the Jews against some of their own brethren. One would certainly have thought that they had had such convincing proof of the folly, to use no harsher term, of endeavouring to compel men by the infliction of disgrace and suffering to adopt or renounce a religious belief, that they would have abstained from such a course themselves. Yet their dealings with the two celebrities of this age, Uriel da Costa and Baruch Spinoza, exhibit an amount of harshness and injustice which their own persecutors could hardly have exceeded.

Both these men were of Portuguese extraction, and belonged to families which went by the name of New Christians. Both were remarkable for great mental activity and an unusually speculative turn of mind. This natural tendency was doubtless fostered by their own early experience—the truth or falsehood of every dogma of their belief having been, as it were, forced upon them as a matter of logical inquiry. It required little knowledge of human nature to understand that the opinions entertained by men like these could be influenced only by calm reasoning and reflection. Yet a course was pursued towards them which could only have been successful in the instance of the weakest or the most timid of men.

Uriel da Costa had belonged to a family of Maranaos, or New Christians, in Spain, where he had not only professed Christianity, but had been ordained a priest. Like so many of his countrymen, he had fled from Spain, and at Amsterdam threw off his pretended belief. But his early experiences had taught him distrust; and he was not disposed to acquiesce implicitly in the Rabbinical interpretation of the Scriptures. After a protracted controversy he composed a work, which he entitled *An Examination of Pharisaical Tradition*. The book does not appear to have been published, or even printed, but was circulated in manuscript among the members of the Jewish community. An eminent Rabbi, Samuel da Silva, took up the controversy, and published a reply to Da Costa's work, which he called *A Treatise on the Immortality of the Soul*. To this Uriel replied by a review of his own essay, enlarged by a refutation of Da Silva's argument. This gave great offence, and severe measures were taken. He was thrown into prison, on the charge of having denied the immortality of the soul. He was with difficulty released, on condition of paying a heavy fine, and suppressing the obnoxious writings. The effect of this harshness was, not to silence, but rather to provoke him to more determined antagonism. He was soon publicly excommunicated, and became, both in opinion and practice, a pronounced Deist. But, after fifteen years of suffering, wearied out by a controversy in which he found himself forsaken by all his friends, he twice sought a reconciliation with his synagogue. Now was the time when he might have been won from his errors. Tenderness and mercy would probably have had their effect on a nature which had much that was noble and generous intermingled with its pride and virulence. But unhappily a different course was pursued. On the second occasion he only obtained readmission to communion by consenting to undergo a public scourging in the synagogue,[184] the shame and degradation of which so affected him that a few days afterwards he destroyed himself.

Da Costa's history has doubtless its moral lesson and its melancholy interest. But in neither particular can it compare with that of Spinoza. In a work like this, neither a lengthened biography of this man nor an analysis of his philosophy can be inserted. Nevertheless, considering the vast influence which his peculiar opinions have had on modern thought,[185] he cannot be dismissed without some notice.

He was born at Amsterdam in 1632. His father had emigrated from Lisbon some years previously, driven thence by religious persecution. Young Spinoza was instructed in Hebrew literature by Mosteira, Chief Rabbi of his synagogue, and in Latin by Van Ende, a physician, for whom he conceived a warm affection. He soon grew dissatisfied with his teachers; and, his revolt from Rabbinical authority attracting notice, remonstrances and threats followed. These failing of effect, he was publicly excommunicated,[186] and his life attempted. Thereupon he retired to Rhynsburg, where he supported himself by grinding optical glasses. Afterwards he removed to Voorburg, and again to the Hague. At all these places he led a quiet, studious, very pure and beautiful life, keeping up a correspondence with some of the greatest philosophers of the day, and more than once refusing offers of advancement. No man was more highminded or unselfish. His favourite pupil, De Vries, who knew that his own hours were numbered, proposed to make Spinoza his heir. But De Vries had a brother living, and Spinoza insisted that the money should be left to him. At his father's death his sisters claimed the whole property, on the ground of Spinoza's excommunication. Spinoza vindicated his right in a court of law, but voluntarily gave up the property in dispute. He died, as calmly as he had lived, of consumption, a.d. 1677, in the forty-fifth year of his age.

No man has ever been more fiercely assailed or more enthusiastically defended. He has been denounced as an Atheist, a Pantheist, a blasphemer, and a fatalist. He has been upheld as a man eminently holy, a devout lover of God and of Christ.[187] Strange as it may seem, all these statements may be said to be true, though of course in different senses of the terms employed. For his Atheism—he seems to have been repelled, from the first, by the anthropomorphism of the Scriptures. It was not merely that God was there represented as possessed of an eye, a hand, etc., but as performing human actions, and influenced by human feelings. This was, in his view, absolute falsehood,[188] and the result was that he entirely rejected the God of revelation, and with Him, of course, the whole scheme of salvation as propounded in the Bible. Thus, then, he may be styled an Atheist. But, on the other hand, he constructed a system in which he affirmed that there exists but one substance, though with infinite attributes, and that this substance is God, who is either absolutely or in some modified form everything. The man who holds this cannot, it may be said, be an Atheist.[189] He is, again, no Pantheist, for he distinguishes between God and the universe;[190] yet the Christian Pantheists, as they may be called, claim him as their own, if not their founder. For the other charges, he no doubt affirms that, as nothing can be done, either directly or indirectly, except by God, all human acts, however wicked, may be said to be done by Him. This, according to our ideas, is both blasphemy and fatalism. Yet Spinoza attributes the *act* only, not its moral wickedness, to God. When pressed to say whether the atrocious murder of Agrippina by Nero was due to God, he answered that it must be so due, so far as the act was concerned. But no act is good or evil in itself, and it was Nero's evil mind, not God's, that made the crime.[191] So with his fatalism.

When he denies that man can act otherwise than as God wills, he appears to enunciate the plainest fatalism;[192] nor do I see how any other conclusion can logically be drawn from his premises. But then Spinoza also teaches the beauty, the happiness, the necessity of holiness, of moral culture and self-discipline—things not merely inconsistent, but irreconcilable, with fatalism. He holds language which an apostle might endorse. 'Justice and charity,' he writes, 'are the one infallible sign of the catholic faith, the genuine fruits of the Holy Spirit. Where they are found, there is Christ. Where they are wanting, Christ is not. For by the Spirit of Christ are we led to justice and charity.' We are led—so, too, the Scriptures teach—led, if we will follow; not blindly driven, as the fatalist must believe.

On the whole, a wise man will hardly speak otherwise than with respect and tenderness of Spinoza. No doubt, notwithstanding the depth and acuteness of his intellect, in which respects he has never probably been exceeded by any of human kind, his system is full of inconsistencies, and has little practical value. How could it be otherwise, when he has attempted that which Revelation itself has with difficulty effected? But he was honest, patient, humble, beneficent, as few men have been; and his desire to attain to truth was earnest and unselfish. As in the case of pious heathens, like Aurelius, we cannot be sure that Christianity was ever put before him in its true aspect. The frivolities of the Talmud, the traditions of the Inquisition, the Church of Roderic Borgia and his successors—were none of them likely to lead him to Christ, as revealed in His blessed Word. Let our sentence on him be, what every good man says of those whom he respects, and yet from whom he is constrained to differ: 'Cum talis sis, utinam noster esses.'[193]

Besides the eminent writers of this century already mentioned, Da Costa, Spinoza, Orobio da Castro, Thomas—or, as he is called by his countrymen, Isaac—de Pinedo, one of the most eminent Greek scholars of the day, deserves mention not only for his classical learning, but for the unusually mild and charitable tone he uniformly employs when speaking of the religion of Christ. To this date also belong David Lara, the lexicographer; Benjamin Musafia, the naturalist; and Isaac Uziel, Emanuel Gomez, and Enrique Enriquez, the poets.

In the earlier part of the century considerable numbers of Jews sailed for the Brazils from the various ports of Holland, under the leadership of two Rabbins, to found a Jewish colony. It throve and attained a considerable amount of prosperity until, in 1654, the Portuguese obtained possession of Brazil. Under these new masters, free exercise of their religion was not allowed the Jews. They therefore quitted the country, some returning to Holland, others settling in Cayenne or Surinam.

FOOTNOTES:

[183] The Sephardim and the Ashkenazim, as indeed is the case in other countries also.

[184] It is added that he was afterwards compelled to lie on the ground, while the whole of the congregation walked over him.

[185] All the great modern thinkers speak with reverence of Spinoza, with the single exception, perhaps, of Leibnitz. Lessing was one of the first to recognise his profound ability. S. T. Coleridge and Goethe express the greatest admiration for him, the latter affirming that he was one of his three great teachers. Later, Herder, Schleiermacher, Hegel, and others have spoken to the same effect. But though his opinions have exercised a wide and most important influence on the minds of others, he has established no school of adherents to his own peculiar philosophy. It may be doubted whether he ever made one genuine convert.

[186] The sentence of excommunication against him ran thus: 'Cursed be he by day, and cursed be he by night; cursed in going out, and cursed in coming in. And we warn you, that none may speak with him by word of mouth, nor by writing, nor show any favour to him, nor be under one roof with him, nor come within four cubits of him, nor read anything written or composed by him.' And this sentence was pronounced by men who had themselves experienced the enormities of religious persecution!

[187] Some have declared him to have been actually a Christian. But though certain passages in his writings may seem to favour that idea, his unhesitating rejection of the doctrine of the Incarnation renders it impossible.

[188] It should be here observed that the Scriptures do not teach anthropomorphism of any kind as actually true, but as the only mode by which man, in the bounded and darkened condition of his intellect, during his present state of being, can apprehend God at all. The Scriptures contain the most distinct denials of anthropomorphism, considered otherwise than as metaphor. Thus, Exod. xxxiii. 20: 'Thou canst not see My face, for there shall no man see Me, and live,' *i.e.*, 'He must be wholly *out of the body*, in order to apprehend Me' —

apprehend Me, that is, with the eye of the spirit, not of the body. See the use of the two words expressing bodily and spiritual vision (John i. 18; John xvi. 16; Rev. iv. 2, etc.). Again, 'God is not a man, that He should lie,' or 'that He should repent' (Num. xxiii. 19). In the anthropomorphic images of Scripture, 'God is seen only through a glass, *darkly*,' as St. Paul says.

[189] We have in more than one of his writings a distinct denial of his Atheism. 'His critics,' he says, 'do not know him, or they would not so easily have persuaded themselves that he taught Atheism.' See also his Treatise, *De Deo et Homine.*

[190] 'Those,' he says also in the same epistle, 'who would identify matter with God *totâ errant viâ.*'

[191] It is again proper to remark that this theory is wholly untenable. The operations of the human will are as much acts, as the operations of the human hand. Nero, if Spinoza's view were correct, could be no more free mentally to conceive wickedness, contrary to God's will, than he was free manually to perpetrate it.

[192] There are, indeed, passages in his works where he denies, or seems to deny, the free will of God Himself.

[193] 'In Spinoza,' says an eminent historian of the Jews, 'were to be found the seeds of a Pascal, if he could only have received Christianity, of which, indeed, he always spoke with respect.' But he had no faith in it, and is only one more illustration of St. Paul's saying: 'Without faith it is impossible to please God.'

CHAPTER XXXV
A.D. 1600-1700. THE JEWS IN SPAIN, ENGLAND, AND ITALY

Few words will suffice to relate what befell the Spanish and Portuguese Jews during this century. Beyond the fact, already recorded, of their oft-recurring migration from both countries to the friendly shelter offered by Holland, there is little to tell. Those who lingered behind, unable or unwilling to quit the land of their birth, continued to practise the old deception, and, when discovered or suspected, to undergo the same merciless severities as their fathers had endured. There is no need to repeat the hideous and monotonous tale of their sufferings. The awe and terror with which the Inquisition was regarded were ever on the increase; until notoriously not the common people, not the grandees and nobles only, but the sovereigns themselves, became little better than its instruments. Early in the century Philip III. is related to have been present at the burning of a Jewish girl, and to have been unable to repress some token of natural horror at the sight. This was noticed by the Grand Inquisitor, who, not satisfied with reproving the monarch for his weakness, ordered some of the coward blood to be drawn from his veins, and burned by the public executioner! Later in the century, in 1680, M. Villars, Louis XIV.'s ambassador at the Court of Spain, describes an Auto da Fé which he witnessed at Madrid, where twenty Jews were publicly burned, with attendant circumstances of revolting barbarity. He relates how the king, Charles II., was present, but occupied a lower seat than that assigned to the Grand Inquisitor.

If we are curious to know what were the sufferings inflicted at the examinations held in the dungeons of the Inquisition, we may learn them from the narrative of Orobio, an eminent Portuguese philosopher and physician. He was suspected of Judaism, and thrown into prison. After some preliminary inquiries, having refused to confess, he was carried, he tells us, into a subterranean vault, dimly lighted, where two officials were seated—the judge and secretary of the Holy Office. He was stripped, strong cords were tied to his hands and feet, the other ends being passed through iron rings in the walls. These were then drawn tight, so that he remained suspended by the cords, which the executioner kept drawing tighter and tighter, until the surgeon certified that further pressure would destroy life. The cords cut into the flesh and made the blood burst from under the nails. He was then told that this was only the beginning of his sufferings, which would be increased in intensity until he confessed. This scene was frequently repeated during three years, at the end of which time, perceiving that his resolution was invincible, they healed his wounds, and permitted him to depart. He fled to Toulouse, and afterwards to Amsterdam, where he threw off his mask, and professed himself a Jew.

Manasseh Ben Israel was another celebrated Portuguese Jew, who was mainly instrumental in the restoration of the Jews to England, from which they had been banished for more than three hundred and fifty years. His father had escaped from the dungeons of the Inquisition at Lisbon, and settled with his family at Amsterdam. He was distinguished as a poet, a philosopher, a physician, and a theologian. His high reputation doubtless was the reason why he was chosen by the Jews at Amsterdam to proceed to England and endeavour to obtain from Oliver Cromwell,—who at that time (a.d. 1656) swayed the destinies of England,—permission for the Jews to return thither. Manasseh presented an address, skilfully drawn, in which he argued that, as regarded both the spiritual and temporal interests of England, it would be to their advantage to grant readmission to the Jews. He asserted that the restoration of Israel was close at hand, and that they who showed kindness to the people of God would be surely rewarded for it in that day. In a secular point of view also, those nations had always been found to flourish most in their undertakings who had sheltered the Jews. He also exploded the calumnies, so often raised against his nation, of crucifying children, and using Christian blood for ritual purposes.[194]

Cromwell received him favourably; but, aware probably of the difficulties with which the question was beset, referred the matter to an assembly of twenty-three persons, whom he appointed to consider the question. Of these, seven were merchants, two lawyers, and the remaining fourteen divines. He himself presided, and opened the debate with an address which those who heard it declared to be one of the ablest and most eloquent he had ever delivered. They had first to consider, he said, whether the admission of the Jews would be legal, and secondly, whether it would be expedient. The lawyers present having at once decided that there would be no illegality, he proceeded to the other question. But here there was much difference of opinion. The citizens were divided as to the alleged commercial advantages, while the theologians disputed so long and so hotly as to the religious aspect of the question, that Cromwell grew weary, and adjourned the consideration of the matter, so far as the council was concerned, *sine die*. Meanwhile he connived at their resettlement, granting them a kind of special protection. Nearly at the same time a piece of land was granted them as a burial-ground, on a nominal lease of 999 years. Whether this action on the part of the Protector gave offence, or whether it was the effect of mere gossip, the wildest and most ridiculous rumours were circulated on the subject. It was said that the Jews had sent a deputation to England to ascertain whether Cromwell was not himself the Messiah, and that they went to Huntingdon to search out his pedigree; also, that they had made an offer of £500,000, to purchase St. Paul's Cathedral for their synagogue, Henry Martin and Hugh Peters being the persons who were to conduct this negotiation. It may be mentioned, in connection with these strange rumours, that Harrington, in his *Oceana* (a.d. 1656), gravely proposes to relieve the Government of the difficulties which the management of Ireland caused them by selling that island to the Jews.

It does not appear that any public measures were taken respecting the Jews during the remainder of Cromwell's government. We have seen that, though their residence in England was a breach of a law still in force, it was not likely that it would be very rigidly insisted on, unless where persons were obnoxious on other grounds; and Cromwell's friendly feeling towards them would of course render their position more secure. It is likely that they came back singly or in small numbers, and were allowed to establish themselves without molestation during the next few years. Then, in the sixth year after the Restoration, some agitation having been raised respecting their presence in England, formal permission was given them by Charles II. to reside in Great Britain, together with liberty of commerce and worship. It is not unlikely that this concession was made to gratify Antonio Mendez, physician to the King of Spain, and his brother Andrea, chamberlain to the Infanta Catherine of Portugal, Charles's queen. It is certain that the brothers about this time came to England, where they settled, resuming their real name of De Costa. Some years afterwards, during the reign of James II., the Jews obtained a remission of the alien duty, which had been imposed on their traffic. This was, however, again exacted in the ensuing reign.

At the accession of William III., when money was wanted for the prosecution of the war in Ireland, it was proposed to require a subsidy of one hundred thousand pounds from the Jews, taking a leaf out of the book of the old Norman kings. But the times were changed. The Jews protested, with an eye, doubtless, to similar exactions to follow, that they would rather leave the country than comply; and they could not now be shut up in prison, and put on the rack, and suffer the daily extraction of their teeth until they paid it. The statesmen of the day perceived that it was simple pillage, and withdrew the proposal.

The days of barbarous and cruel violence had indeed passed away, and happily for ever. It is perhaps a fortunate circumstance,—grave as were the injuries resulting to both parties from it,—that the Jews were absent from England for so long a period. The tradition of persecution had, in consequence, long been broken off. In Spain, in Portugal, in Germany, even in Holland and Italy, people still living had themselves witnessed,—or had heard from their fathers,—the imprisonments, the expulsions, and the massacres of the Jews on the occasion of some religious excitement. But the fires of persecution had been cold for centuries in England, and no one was inclined to rekindle them now, even had it been possible to do so.[195]

In Italy, throughout the seventeenth century, the condition of the Jews seems to have been fairly prosperous. Little is related of them, and that is the best evidence that they were exempt from injustice and persecution. Of the ten occupants of the papal chair during this century, the only one who seems to have interfered much in their affairs was Innocent XI., and his dealings with them, as we shall presently see, were lenient and friendly. It is said that at the outset of the century there were more than a hundred synagogues of the Jews in the Italian cities. In those situated on the sea-coast the commerce was, to a great extent, in the hands of the Hebrews, and their wealth was continually on the increase. Jews also continued to be employed in diplomatic missions by the Italian governments—by the Republic of Venice, the Dukes of Ferrara, and even by the Emperor. The same, indeed, was the case all over Europe. The kings of Denmark, Sweden, and Prussia,—nay, even of Spain and Portugal, notwithstanding their implacable persecution of the Jewish nation,—were in the habit of employing Jews as their emissaries. Sir William Temple, who was English ambassador at the Hague in 1668, expresses his astonishment at this fact. The Baron de Belmont was the Spanish minister in Holland during the whole of the latter half of the seventeenth century, and Nunez da Costa held a similar office under the crown of Portugal, though both these were notoriously Jews.

In literary eminence the Italian Jews of this century are said to be inferior both to the generations which preceded and those which followed them. This is attributed to the severe censorship of the press, which is always unfavourable to literature. The famous Leo of Modena, head of the synagogue of Venice, and author of many works, both in Italian and Hebrew, on antiquities and theology, is an instance of this. He was on the point, we are told, of making a translation of the Hebrew Scriptures into Italian, which would have been beyond doubt a valuable work, but the Inquisition commanded him to desist.

But if their writings were handled with severity, the same cannot be said of their persons. It is mentioned, indeed, that in Rome, during the pontificate of Innocent XI., they were in such favour with the people that their synagogues were frequented by the latter, and in such numbers that the Pope was obliged to threaten his subjects with excommunication, and a fine of twenty crowns every time they resorted to a place of Jewish worship.

The same pontiff was very earnest for their conversion. He built seminaries where Jews might receive instruction in the Christian faith, and houses where such as had become converts might be maintained. He caused sermons to be preached, in which it was proved from the Hebrew Scriptures that Jesus Christ was the Messiah whom they expected. In order to encourage still further proselytes to the Christian faith, some person of high rank, a nobleman or a cardinal, stood godfather to them on the occasion of their baptism. A handsome present in money also was made them: they were dressed in white satin, and carried about Rome in fine coaches for a fortnight afterwards, receiving everywhere the congratulations of the spectators. At the same time it was very plainly intimated to them, that if they relapsed into Judaism they would straightway be burnt alive.[196]

It is certainly strange that under such circumstances conversions were not effected. Innocent evinced not only the controversial zeal which many before and after him have shown, but also an amount of real charity and goodwill which must, one would have thought, have had a very potent influence with the Jews of that day. When the Venetians, in 1685, after their successful war in the Morea, brought back a large number both of Christian and Jewish captives, they gave the former their freedom, but retained the latter in servitude. Innocent, however, interfered, and insisted on their liberating the Jews also. But we learn that, notwithstanding all his generous exertions on their behalf, he failed in making any considerable number of real converts. Cardinal Barberini who had spent large sums and used great exertions in endeavouring to accomplish this work, was compelled to own that the conversions had been for the most part insincere. It is not, indeed, by such means as those employed that converts can be made.

As regards the distinguished literary men of this period, it has already been remarked that there were fewer of these than in previous and subsequent generations; and, in the majority of European nations, such as there were do not contrast favourably with either their predecessors or successors. There were, however, writers of genius and learning; among them Solomon Norzi, of Mantua, is the author of a celebrated Massoretic work which, though it was not published till a century after his death, has attained a great reputation. The two Aboabs, both residents in Venice, were celebrated for their writings: the former, Emmanuel by name, being the author of an able work on tradition; the latter chiefly remarkable for his exposure of the impious impostures of the pretended prophet, Sabbathai

Sevi. Judah da Modena produced many greatly admired works, and, in particular, a Hebrew lexicon, and a *System of Artificial Memory*. Solomon Medigo, physician to Prince Radziwill at Wilna, and Moses Luzzato, of Venice, should also be mentioned.

FOOTNOTES:

[194] Manass. *Vindiciæ Judaicæ*. See Appendix V.

[195] Manasseh did not live to see the success of his efforts on behalf of his countrymen. He died on his journey back to Holland, in 1657.

[196] Throughout this and the succeeding century, and, indeed, for fully half of the present century, however much the stern rigour of previous ages of persecution may have been relaxed, the condition of the Jews was miserable in the extreme. They were strictly confined to their Ghetto, the gates of which were closed regularly every evening at eight o'clock, and such Jews as had not returned by that time were obliged to remain outside all night. In front of a small church standing near the entrance of the Ghetto was fixed a large wooden crucifix, highly coloured and gilded, with the inscription, 'All day long have I stretched forth Mine hands to a disobedient and gainsaying people.' Into this church the Jews at one time were driven with scourges, by order of the popes, to listen to sermons preached against their obstinacy and rebellion.

CHAPTER XXXVI
A.D. 1600-1700. THE JEWS IN
THE EAST.—SABBATHAI SEVI

The condition of the Jews in the East during this century does not call for much remark; indeed, little has been recorded respecting it. The treatment they received at the hands of the Mussulmans, both princes and people, was curiously different from that which they experienced from the Christian populations of Europe. The first named did not regard the Jews with any particular favour or respect,—in fact, the disdain they evinced for them was even greater than that entertained by their Christian contemporaries,—but there was no *active* enmity. They looked on with scornful indifference while the Israelites plied their busy trade, aware though they might be that the wealth they accumulated was in a great measure drawn from their own coffers. They would spit in contempt as they passed a Jewish synagogue, but they would not raise a finger to cause its demolition or prevent any number of worshippers from crowding into it. All over Turkey, Arabia, and Persia, some Jews were to be found in every town, where they were allowed to live and thrive, unless they broke some law or offended some faithful Islamite. But if they did either of these things, they were apt to experience scant ceremony and sharp punishment.

The reader has heard, in a previous chapter, of the massacre perpetrated by Shah Abbas II., which appears to have occurred about a.d. 1666. It is said to have lasted three years, and to have almost exterminated the Jews in his dominions. It is, however, involved in great obscurity, the dates given by different writers varying considerably. But in this year, 1666, not the Jews of the East only, but all over the world, were greatly excited by the appearance of the most persistent and successful impostor that had arisen among them from the time of Barchochebas. Sabbathai Sevi, a native of Smyrna, and son of a poulterer in that city, was born in 1625. He was sent to school, where he made such rapid progress that he was appointed a Rabbi when he was only eighteen years of age. He early attracted attention and had many followers, who believed in the pretensions which, even then, he put forward, of being the expected Messiah. At the age of twenty he married a woman of great beauty and rank; but the marriage was only a nominal one, as he lived entirely apart from her. He was compelled to give a divorce, and soon afterwards made a second similar marriage, with the same result. He practised strict asceticism, fasting six days in every week, and bathing continually in the sea at midnight. At twenty-four, his reputation had increased so greatly, that he ventured to put forth publicly his pretensions to be thought the Messiah, and, in proof of these, ventured to pronounce publicly the name of Jehovah, which is absolutely forbidden to the Jews. The Rabbins were horror-struck at his impiety, and declared him to be worthy of death. He was compelled to fly from Smyrna, and took refuge in one city after another, until in Gaza he made an important proselyte, the celebrated Nathan Benjamin. This man, a person of position and influence, professed to have seen in a vision the Lord Himself; who informed him that the promised Deliverer had come in the person of Sabbathai Sevi, and that he, Nathan Benjamin, was the Elias who was to herald his coming. The reader will remember that this is the exact repetition of the imposture of Barchochebas and Rabbi Akiba, fifteen hundred years before. Aided by this ally, Sabbathai preached in Jerusalem, and resided for thirteen years in that city, continuing to gain proselytes and bearing down all opposition.

The imposture was aided by the remarkable fact that, according to the interpretation of some eminent Cabalists of a passage in the book of the prophet Daniel, the Messiah would make His appearance about the year 1675. One of Nathan Benjamin's first steps, when he felt himself strong enough to take it, was to assemble the Jews resident in Jerusalem, and inform them that, by virtue of the authority committed to him from on high, he abrogated the fast which would otherwise be observed in the ensuing June, because the time of the coming of the Messiah was a festal one, inconsistent with mourning of any kind. He then brought Sabbathai out to them, who, he said, in the ensuing November would go forth in power and destroy the Ottoman empire. He encountered determined opposition from the wiser among his countrymen, who perceived that his pretensions were not only without foundation, but were likely to bring the gravest calamities on the Jews everywhere throughout the Sultan's dominions. They even went so far as to try him as a rebel and an impostor, and condemn him to death. His adherents, however, were too many and too powerful to permit of this sentence being carried into effect, and he continued to reside without molestation in the city.

After a period of thirteen years from the date of this announcement of his pretensions, he made an expedition into Egypt, where he married, for the third time, the daughter of a Polish Jew, who professed to have received a revelation that she was the destined bride of the Messiah. But the marriage, like the two former ones, was only a marriage in name; and

Sabbathai returned to Jerusalem, where he resided for three years more, and then publicly proclaimed himself in one of the synagogues as the Messiah. This once more roused the indignation of the Rabbins, who pronounced against him the sentence of excommunication. This sentence he found too strong for him to struggle against, and he fled to his native city, Smyrna.

The report of his condemnation had preceded him; but he was nevertheless welcomed in his native city with almost regal honour. Every evening he paraded the streets, accompanied by a train of followers, carrying banners, and singing hymns in his praise. All resistance offered to him proved vain. A Jew of high rank, named Anakia, attacked him in the market-place, branding him as an impostor. But his fate did not encourage others to pursue the same course. He returned to his home, and had scarcely entered it, when he suddenly fell from his chair a corpse. The reader will not require to be told that Sabbathai's friends declared this to be God's judgment on the blasphemer!

His pretensions now rose higher.[197] He assumed the state of a monarch. He divided the kingdoms of the earth among his partisans. He named his two brothers sovereigns of Judah and Israel, while he himself took the title of 'the King of the Kings of the Earth.' He ordered the name of the Sultan to be removed from the prayer offered up for the sovereign in the Jewish liturgy, and his own to be inserted in its place. Embassies arrived from foreign communities charged with rich presents and assurances of devoted loyalty. These were sometimes kept waiting two or three weeks for an audience. His picture was exhibited in public, surmounted by a golden crown; and multitudes of prophets of both sexes thronged the streets, declaring in the name of Heaven his approaching triumph. Some of these are said to have acquired in a moment a miraculous knowledge of Hebrew!

It was not in Smyrna only, or in its vicinity, that the madness prevailed. In those European cities in which the largest number of Jews were to be found,—Hamburg, and Frankfort, and Amsterdam,—all other topics of interest were postponed, and business was broken off to discuss the doings of the newly risen Prophet of Israel. The excitement was not less in the East, where the husbandmen are related to have refused to do their ordinary work in the fields, because the Deliverer of Israel had come. If Sabbathai had been really a man of ability and courage, there is no saying what he might not have effected. It is probable, however, that the extraordinary amount of success to which he had attained now embarrassed, rather than gratified, him. He felt that he could neither recede nor stand still. His partisans insisted on his passing over to Constantinople, and advancing his pretensions in the face of the Sultan himself. He made the voyage accordingly, attended by a vast number of his adherents, and was received by the Jews of Constantinople with the utmost enthusiasm. The Sultan was at the time of his arrival absent, but Sabbathai demanded an audience of the grand vizier. The latter sent immediately to his master for instructions, and delayed giving any reply until he received them. The Sultan's reply was, that Sabbathai was to be arrested and kept in safe custody until his return. First one, and then a second officer of janissaries were accordingly sent; but in the presence of Sabbathai they were so overpowered by awe that they dared not execute their office. Once more, if Sabbathai had had boldness equal to the occasion, he might have made himself master of Constantinople. But he surrendered himself of his own accord, and was kept in a kind of honourable captivity in the castle of Sestos, where, however, his followers were freely permitted to visit him. He put out a manifesto ordering that the fast which was always strictly observed on the anniversary of the destruction of Jerusalem should be suspended, and the day celebrated as a festival, it being the birthday of the Messiah. At this juncture there arrived a learned Cabalist, Rabbi Nehemiah, the head of one of the synagogues in Poland, who took up his abode in the castle as Sabbathai's guest. A few days' intercourse satisfied him that Sabbathai was simply an impostor, and as such he denounced him to his followers. Roused to fury, the partisans of the prophet would have killed him on the spot; but Nehemiah snatched a turban from the head of one of the Turks, and declared himself a Mussulman. The janissaries instantly interfered to protect him, and he was conveyed to Adrianople where he had an interview with the Sultan. The latter now returned to the capital, and summoned Sabbathai to his presence. The impostor in the hour of trial entirely lost the hardihood which he had hitherto displayed, and, when the Sultan demanded of him whether he was the Messiah, could not summon courage to reply. The Sultan proposed to test his pretensions by shooting three poisoned arrows at him. If these failed to wound or injure him, his title should be at once acknowledged; if the result should be different, death or the profession of Mahometanism must be his sentence. Sabbathai did not hesitate. Following the example of Nehemiah, he placed a turban on his head and exclaimed—'There is but one God, and Mahomet is His Prophet!'

It is most extraordinary that this apostasy, evidently the result of mere cowardice and imposture, did not provoke the contempt alike of the Turks and the Jews. But by the Sultan he was loaded with honours, and the Jews did not withdraw their belief in his miraculous pretensions. With unabated impudence he put out a declaration to the effect that God had changed him from an Israelite to an Ishmaelite. He quoted the example of Moses, who dwelt for a time among the Ethiopians, and the fifty-third chapter of Isaiah, where it is said that the Messiah was numbered among the transgressors. For a long time he continued to maintain his double character of the deliverer of the Jews and the devoted believer in Mahomet. Some even declared, after the fashion of the Gnostics in the early Church, that the true Sabbathai had been taken up into heaven, and it was only his likeness or phantom that had undergone degradation and apostasy. Great numbers of Jews, indeed, were induced, by his example, to become Mahometans; and at length the injury to the Jewish community became so great, that they exerted all the influence they could command with the grand vizier, who caused Sabbathai to be arrested and banished into Bosnia. There, in 1676, ten years after his apostasy to Mahometanism, and in the fifty-first year of his age, he expired in a castle near Belgrade. According to some, he died a natural death; according to others, he was beheaded in prison. The latter is the more likely supposition. Though he endeavoured to persuade the Jews that, notwithstanding his profession of another faith, he was at heart a Jew, they entirely distrusted him; and it is likely that the assurances to which they would lend no credit nevertheless caused suspicion and uneasiness among true followers of Mahomet. Thus it would be the interest of both parties to cut short his career.

In the long catalogue of impostors who have succeeded for a time in blinding the eyes of those to whom they pretended a mission, the case of Sabbathai Sevi seems the most extraordinary.

There have been innumerable false Messiahs, from the days of Judas of Galilee almost to our own time; and to each of these in turn the Jews of their day accorded, for the time at least, a ready welcome, which, in almost every instance, ultimately gave place to a total disbelief in their pretensions. In the instance of this man alone, the faith placed in him was not exchanged for contempt and distrust. Yet he was certainly the one among all the pretenders to a Divine mission who most deserved such ignominy. Judas,[198] Barchochebas, David Alroy—however unfounded their claims to be the Messiah—at all events persisted resolutely to the last, and died with the same watchword on their lips that they had uttered during life. But though Sabbathai openly avowed his own imposture, his followers continued to believe in him. More than one prophet arose after his death, and obtained credence by affirming that Sabbathai had been translated into heaven, as Enoch and Elijah before him, and would, after a stated interval, reappear on earth. Sabbathaism, as it was called, became the creed of a powerful and numerous sect, of which we shall hear in the ensuing century. It is said that even now it is not extinct. This example is one proof out of many that human credulity exceeds all bounds of calculation.

Among those who continued to uphold Sabbathai after this fashion long after his death, the most noted were Nehemiah Chajon and Abraham Michael Cardoso. The plea urged by the latter in behalf of his principal may safely be pronounced the most extravagant that has ever been advanced. It was doubtless great wickedness, he said, to apostatize to Islamism; but then it should be remembered that the Messiah was not to come until mankind were all good or all bad. There was no prospect of their all becoming good. So Sabbathai, by his wickedness in accepting Mahomet, was helping on, like a true prophet, the coming of the Messiah!

FOOTNOTES:

[197] He is said to have quoted Isaiah xiv. 14: 'I will ascend above the heights of the clouds,' and to have appealed to his followers to say whether they had not seen him so ascend; to which they made answer that they had! It must be added, however, that, if he did quote the passage in question as applicable to himself, he could hardly have studied its context.

[198] Whether Judas himself ever claimed to be the Messiah is doubtful. But a considerable section of his followers certainly believed him to be such.

CHAPTER XXXVII
A.D. 1700-1800. THE JEWS IN SPAIN, ITALY, AND FRANCE

We enter now on the eighteenth century, and are, as it were, in sight of the history of our own times. The position in which we find the Jews is in the main the same which they at present occupy. In Romish countries they were still liable to sharp persecution, sometimes from mob violence, sometimes from the action of the Church. The lands in which the severest measures were enforced continued to be Spain and Portugal, where the Inquisition was dominant throughout the entire century, though its power gradually but very evidently diminished as the years passed on. In the reign of Philip V., who succeeded to the Spanish throne a.d. 1700, and held it till 1746, the first direct blow was given to its authority. In the War of Succession, which began at the outset of his reign, his French allies treated the Inquisition with very scant respect. They broke open the prisons of the Holy Office, released the prisoners, and even seized the silver images in the Dominican chapels, melting them down to pay the expenses of the campaign. The king took no part in the spoliation; but when the Inquisitors appealed to him against the sacrilegious violence of the French, he replied that he could not interfere with the measures taken by his allies. He was a weak and sombre-tempered young man, though not, it would seem, a religious bigot, and allowed the clergy in the main to have their way. One *Auto da Fé* was held every year throughout his reign; and the number of victims is said to have amounted to 14,000. There can be little doubt that the greater part of these were 'secret Jews.' It is beyond dispute that throughout this century, and long afterwards—even, it is said, to our own times—secret Judaism continued to maintain its hold; and from time to time discoveries were made, and executions followed.

In 1713 the English were confirmed in the possession of Gibraltar, which had been wrested from Spain some ten years before. But it is a singular fact that the Spaniards, even when yielding up their stronghold to Great Britain, could not endure that the Jews should be allowed to live in peace there; and one clause of the treaty stipulated that 'no Jew should be tolerated in that city.'[199]

Ferdinand VI. succeeded his father in 1746, and reigned till 1759. He bears the character of a good and wise prince, and no public *Auto da Fé* took place in his time, though there appear to have been a considerable number of petty local executions. Probably these took place without his sanction, or even knowledge. He died without issue, and was succeeded by his brother, Charles III. He again was an able and vigorous sovereign, and the power of the Inquisition still further diminished during his reign. Three years after his accession he took the decided step of banishing the Grand Inquisitor for encroaching on the privileges of the Crown. In 1770, and again in 1784, he ordered that any procedure against offenders must be approved by the king, and sufficient evidence adduced to justify imprisonment. He was succeeded by his son, Charles IV., the weak and miserable victim of Napoleon's ambition. The Inquisition was upheld during his reign, though it does not appear that any *Auto da Fé* took place. Very much the same is the history of the Jewish persecution in Portugal, the power of the Inquisition, though greatly limited, still subsisting to the very end of the century.

In Italy very nearly the same state of things continued as has been described under the history of the previous century. On the separation of the kingdom of the Two Sicilies from that of Spain, Charles, who succeeded to the sovereignty, reversed the policy which had been pursued by his predecessors, and invited the Jews to settle for sixty years in his kingdom. He offered to confer upon them rights and privileges which would have left them little ground of complaint. They were to be allowed to hold lands, except such as conferred feudal rights on their possessors. They were to be permitted to trade with all parts of the world, exempt from any special impost—on the same terms, in fact, as his Christian subjects. They might practise all professions, that of the physician included, and have Christian patients, if the latter desired it. They might also follow any handicraft; they might serve in the army; they might freely print and circulate their literature; they might have Christians in their service. They were to be free also to build synagogues and celebrate their religious rites; and the authority of their clergy was to be upheld by the State. All men, in fine, were forbidden, under severe penalties, to insult or wrong them; and all attempts to proselytize their children were to be discouraged. We do not wonder at hearing that Jews in great numbers, from all parts of Europe, accepted King Charles's invitation; neither can it move our surprise to hear that his subjects were not inclined to acquiesce in their sovereign's enlightened views. The Pope of the day, Clement XII., and his confessor, a man of great influence in the Church, denounced the concessions made to the Jews; the clergy preached inflammatory sermons from their pulpits, a Capuchin friar publicly warned the king that, as the punishment of his guilty act, he would die childless.

The Jews could not face the storm. They knew that any attempt to open shops, or bring their merchandise into Naples, would be the signal for a riot, not improbably for a massacre. After a brief sojourn in the city, they withdrew from it.

In 1775, Pius VI., the Pope whom Napoleon imprisoned and deposed, revived some of the harsh laws against the Jews, whose condition, for a long time past, had been growing more peaceful and assured. He issued an edict by which Rabbinical literature was suppressed; no Hebrew book, or even manuscript, might remain in the possession of a Jew. He was required to keep himself rigidly within the limits of his Ghetto; he was obliged again to wear his yellow badge; when a corpse was buried, no funeral procession was allowed; no Jew might employ a Christian midwife or wet-nurse; and, *vice versâ*, a Christian might not employ Jews. The old enactment requiring Jews to attend controversial sermons was again enforced; and the Rabbins were obliged to draw up lists of their disciples, who were required to be present. This seems to have been at the outset of Pius's long reign. The outbreak of the French Revolution, and the troubles which it brought upon him, probably gave a new direction to his thoughts.

Turning to France, we find that the condition of the Jews during the eighteenth century was very peculiar. It has been mentioned in a previous chapter that, although nominally excluded from France, they had long been suffered to dwell there under protections granted to them by Henry II. and others. There were, indeed, three different sections of Jews resident in France at this time—the Portuguese Jews, to whom charters were granted by the French Parliament a.d. 1550. These were chiefly to be found in Bayonne, Bordeaux, and its vicinity. They appear at first to have passed under the name of New Christians, and as such, no doubt, were obliged to submit themselves to the ordinances of the Church; but in the fierce strife which ensued between the Catholics and Huguenots they escaped notice. It is said that they contracted marriages according to their own rites, and evaded the baptism of their children. There were, again, the Jews of Avignon, who were either Italians or native Frenchmen. These had been tolerated by the Popes during their residence there, and probably no great notice had been taken of them since the removal of the papal court. Again, after the conquest of Metz and Alsace, a considerable number of German Jews became subjects of France. It is likely that they by no means regretted the change of masters; for only a few years before, the Parliament at Metz had burnt a number of Jews on the old charge of murdering infants. Louis XIV. granted the Jews of Alsace the same privileges possessed by Bordeaux and other cities—that of free commerce, on condition of paying a certain poll-tax, subsequently compounded for a lump sum. Nevertheless, all over Lorraine and Alsace the

Jews, during this century, were harshly dealt with. Their usurious exactions rendered them odious to the people, as indeed had been the case with their ancestors for many generations. In Strasburg only a few Jewish families were allowed to reside. In Lorraine the laws of Duke Leopold, made in 1724, continued long in force. By these only 180 families were permitted to reside and to carry on trade; and even these were required to live within the Jewish quarters.

When the Edict of Nantes was revoked, and all the subjects of the King of France were required to accept the ordinances of the Catholic Church, the Jews in France were in some danger of persecution. But the act seems never to have been carried out so far as they were concerned. As before, the clergy were too busy in enforcing the law against Huguenots to trouble themselves about a handful of Jews. But, though they were kindly treated, it would be a mistake to suppose that they were naturalized, as some writers have affirmed. It is said that they offered the Regent Orleans two million livres in exchange for the privilege of naturalization—a sum which that impecunious potentate would have been well pleased to lay his hands on. But he was afraid of the unpopularity he would incur by the act, and refused the offer. The writer of the pamphlet respecting the Naturalization Bill of 1753, quoted in a previous chapter, says: 'It is a vulgar error to suppose that the Jews in France were naturalized subjects; and any Frenchman of whom you asked the question would laugh in your face.' It appears to have been only in certain cities that the Jews were allowed to reside permanently. In Lyons they could only reside three months consecutively. In Paris it is said their residence was altogether prohibited.

Louis XV. appears to have treated them with kindness, and to have discouraged a step which was made to abridge their privileges. He also showed much favour to the celebrated Samuel Bernard, the famous banker of his day, who afterwards became a convert to the Church. As the century advanced, and Voltaire and the Encyclopædists began to exercise a wide influence in France, it might have been expected that they would have exerted it in favour of the Jews; who, although they were no longer exposed to the terrible sufferings they had undergone in previous generations, were still subject to a more modified religious persecution—a thing utterly abhorrent to the writers in question. But the Encyclopædists disliked the Jews almost as much as the Christians. The Hebrew race had suffered cruelly in previous ages, as being the enemies of the Gospel. But in the eyes of the infidel writers they were almost as objectionable, as being the living witnesses of its truth. No Dominican persecutor of the fifteenth century would have viewed the Jews with more contempt and hatred than does Voltaire, the advocate of religious tolerance.

In fact, it is obvious that the Jews had to undergo many hardships in France during the reigns of Louis XIV. and XV. A few years after the accession of Louis XVI., the mildness of whose temper had become generally known, a petition was presented by the Jews to the king and council, complaining of the heavy burdens laid upon them. Besides the fees exacted for the royal protection, a capitation tax was imposed upon them by the feudal superior on whose estate they resided. The right of residence was only personal, and a fresh sum had to be paid for every child that was born to them. Further, a toll was paid by every Jew at the gate of every city which he entered, as though he had been a horse or a sheep. There were besides restrictions on their commerce, which weighed heavily upon them.

The appeal to Louis XVI. was not in vain. The obnoxious capitation tax was abolished in 1784; and in 1788 a commission was appointed, of which Malesherbes was the president, and the first act of the latter was to put an end to the toll at the city gates.[200] Malesherbes also set on foot measures for ameliorating generally the condition of the Jews. He proposed to give a prize for the best essay on the subject. This was gained by the celebrated Abbé Grégoire, whose essay was very generally approved. Steps were taken to carry out some of the improvements suggested. But before this could be done the Revolution had begun, and liberty, equality, and fraternity for all men had become the general cry in France. The Jews were not slow to avail themselves of their opportunity, and sent in their petition to the General Assembly to be admitted to the rights of equal citizenship. The question was discussed in the National Assembly, and was affirmed, though not until after considerable debate. On the 17th of September, 1791, the decree was passed by which Jews, without exception or distinction, were admitted to the rights of French citizenship. It was ratified also by the Constitution of 1795.

FOOTNOTES:

[199] This was soon set aside, being contrary to the spirit of English law. The Jews established themselves in Gibraltar, and are now a thriving population, with four synagogues.

[200] The tariff of tolls has been preserved, and has a curious sound. For a Jew 12 deniers (about 1d.), a Jewess and child 9 deniers, a Jewess 6 deniers; for a dead Jew 5 sous, a dead Jewess 30 deniers.

CHAPTER XXXVIII
A.D. 1700-1800. THE JEWS IN GERMANY AND CENTRAL EUROPE

The condition of the Jews in Germany, Prussia, and Austria, at the outset of the eighteenth century, was, if we may believe the historians of the time, an unusually wretched one. The accounts given by the eminent German Jew, J. M. Jost, of the sufferings of his countrymen at that period, cannot fail to move the reader's compassion.[201] 'They were,' to use his own phrase, 'a heap of suffering.' Insult and wrong had, indeed, for many an age, been their portion—a fact to which every history of them that has been written bears melancholy witness. In many countries of Europe, however, the period succeeding the Reformation had brought some amelioration of their condition. But in the countries which we have now under consideration, the Jews had sunk, if it was possible, to a lower position than they had occupied before. Their miseries had, in truth, endured so long, that they had become almost insensible to them. The favourite German proverb, which was current for many centuries, may by itself serve to show the light in which they were regarded. 'Happy is that town,' was the saying, 'in which there is neither a Jew, a tyrant, nor a leper.'

To begin with Prussia. We have seen how, in 1670, the Jews had been driven by Leopold I. out of Vienna, and had found a refuge in Prussia; which the humanity of Frederick William, who, on account of his wisdom and piety, obtained the popular title of 'the Great Elector,' had accorded them. His son, Frederick I., lay under obligations to Gompertz and Elias, two Jews who had been of great service to him in providing him with resources in carrying on the war in which he was engaged. When the Jews had been driven out of Austria, they employed these two men to plead their cause; and the result was, that a certain number of Jewish families were allowed to establish themselves in Berlin, Potsdam, and other cities of the Electoral State. From this permission the whole history of the Prussian Jews may be said to date. The action of the Elector produced considerable discontent among his subjects; but the Elector was firm, and a few years afterwards a special body of rules for the Jews of the electorate was drawn up and put in force. It was, on the whole, extremely favourable to them, though they were still excluded from all public offices, and freedom to worship according to their own creed was not allowed them. But soon afterwards, some Jews, who were the court jewellers, obtained permission to hold religious services in their own private houses. This was a step towards allowing a synagogue to be built, in which public worship was offered; but the ritual, we are told, underwent the strictest examination, to make sure that it did not contain anything insulting to Christianity. In 1712, the king prohibited, under severe penalties, the influx of wandering Jews into the country—a measure which, though it might seem to be unfriendly to the Jewish people, was in reality of the greatest benefit to the respectable portion of them. During Frederick William's reign also, a splendid synagogue—the finest, it was said, in that day in all Germany—was built and opened under the royal sanction, notwithstanding the outcry that the concession provoked.

In 1717, King Frederick died, and was succeeded by Frederick William, the father and predecessor of Frederick the Great. He was a sovereign of the most despotic character, though neither cruel nor unjust. His characteristic qualities were displayed in his dealings with the Jews. He continued the privileges granted to them by his father—indeed, added some others. But, on the other hand, he imposed upon them some rather arbitrary burdens, which, however, savour more of eccentricity than harshness. Thus, if the king at his hunting parties killed more wild boars or stags than he could consume at his own table, the Jews were obliged to purchase what remained. It is said that the Jews, unable to eat up the venison themselves, made a present of it to the public hospitals. Again, on the occasion of any event of importance in a family, such as succession to an inheritance, the birth of an heir, the marriage of a son, etc., every Jew was obliged to make purchases to the amount of three hundred thalers at the royal porcelain factory. Towards the end of the century, during the reign of Frederick William II., they were released from this obligation on paying down the lump sum of four thousand thalers.

In 1740, Frederick William died, and his son, who bears in history the name of 'the Great,' succeeded to the throne. His dealings with the Jews were very peculiar. He had no predilection for them; indeed, whatever personal feeling he entertained for them was of an opposite character. The friend and pupil of Voltaire, he shared that philosopher's prejudice against them. They were no friends of Christianity, to be sure; but they were the religious ancestors of the Christians, the strongest witnesses of the truth of the Gospel, and as such odious in his eyes. On the other hand, there was a grim sense of justice discernible even in his strange legislation respecting them; and, independently of this, he was shrewd enough to see that persecution of them was by no means a profitable policy. 'No one ever got any good by injuring that nation,' was his observation on one occasion. Indeed, his legislation seems to have been designed more for the purpose of preventing the increase of their numbers, than for exacting severe imposts or restricting their civil privileges. Thus, in 1750, the edict he issued for the regulation of the Jews in his dominions draws a strict distinction between the Jews that are tolerated by inheritance and those that are personally tolerated—where the toleration, that is to say, does not descend to the children of the person to whom it is granted. To the latter class belonged all those who were not directly engaged in trade, or did not hold any post or office in a synagogue. Among those who were tolerated by inheritance, the privilege of domicile descended to one child only. Subsequently, in consideration of the payment of seventy thousand thalers, the privilege was extended to a second child, though he could only enjoy it on producing evidence that he was in possession of a property of one thousand thalers. A foreign Jew could not settle in Prussia, unless he paid an exorbitant price for his admission. If the widow of a protected Jew married one who was not so protected, she was obliged to leave the country. Besides these burdens, and of course the ordinary taxes paid by all the king's subjects, there were several imposts. There was a patent of protection whenever a child was born, a tax upon every marriage, and upon the election of every elder of a synagogue. The Jew was also excluded from all civil offices, from agriculture, from keeping an inn, a brewery, or a distillery, from setting up a manufactory of any kind, or from practising the profession of a physician or a surgeon. All Jewish servants who wished to marry were obliged to leave the country. Finally, the Jews were interdicted from acquiring house property, unless they had the express permission of the king. In no case could a Jew possess more than forty houses.

In 1786, Frederick William II., the nephew of Frederick the Great, succeeded to his uncle's throne. He was a wise and merciful sovereign, and he endeavoured to ameliorate the condition of the Jews, partly by mitigating the rigour of existing laws, partly by enacting new ones. Since his time, the state of things has gradually but surely improved. But the legislation of those times, as an intelligent writer has remarked, 'bears the stamp of the fearfully degraded state of the Jewish population, and of the oppressive, exclusive, and repressive measures which were thought needful to the interests of that portion of the community.'[202]

The position of the Jews in the Austrian dominions, in the early part of the eighteenth century, was no better than in Prussia. The Emperor Charles VII. entertained a dislike to them, which induced him to listen readily to any enemy who traduced them. The same was the case to perhaps a greater extent with the Empress Maria Theresa, his daughter. A few years after her accession she decreed the banishment of all the Jews in her dominions, amounting, it is believed, to two hundred thousand persons. A considerable number did take their departure; and the rest would have had to follow, if the intercession of the English and Dutch Governments had not induced her to forego her purpose. Subsequently she relaxed the severity of her dealings with them. She not only permitted their residence, but allowed them to follow certain trades, as, for example, dealing in jewels, or opening shops as money-changers or manufacturers. They were permitted to carry on their services in their synagogues, though they were strictly confined to their houses on Sundays, especially during the hours when Christian worship was going on.

When Joseph II. came into full possession of the imperial power, by the death of his mother in 1780, one of his first acts was to publish an edict of toleration, by which the status of the Jews was greatly improved. All the old prohibitive regulations were annulled. The Jews were at liberty to take up their abode in any town throughout the Austrian dominions, and in the country also—though, in that case, they were required to seek the Emperor's permission. He also opened to them the schools and universities throughout the empire, allowing them to take degrees as doctors in medicine, civil law, and moral philosophy; but he obliged them to open elementary schools of their own for the preparation of their children to enter those belonging to the State. He allowed them to follow any trade they fancied, with the single exception of the manufacture of gunpowder. They were free also to attend the public markets and fairs throughout the country, to wear what apparel they pleased, to occupy any house in any quarter of the towns, and use the public promenades as freely as the other inhabitants. They might also enter the army—indeed, after a while, they became liable to the conscription—and might be made non-commissioned officers; but as, according to the military code of Austria, none can hold commissions who are not of noble blood, they could rise no higher. Lastly, their children were protected against proselytism, it being unlawful to attempt inducing them to change their religion until they had passed their fourteenth year. This edict may be regarded as marking a new era in Jewish history; and whatever amelioration may have taken place in European legislation, so far as they are concerned, in reality dates from it.

In 1781 Councillor Dohm published his famous treatise 'on the amendment of the political position of the Jews.' This writer upholds the principle of bestowing liberty and equality of rights on the Jews, of their free admission to schools and colleges belonging to the State, of their unfettered practice of trades and professions, and even of their participation in public offices of trust. But he contends that the authority of the Rabbins over their congregations, their infliction of discipline, and, under some circumstances, of excommunication, must be upheld by the State. The publication of the work excited a good deal of angry feeling among the German Jews. The renowned Moses Mendelssohn, of whom we shall speak in the next chapter, published a letter respecting it, in which he denounced the spiritual tyranny of the Rabbins in indignant language, which had a very wide and important effect on his countrymen.

In Russia, during this century, the position of the Jews was fully as miserable as in any European country. It has been already pointed out, that by the strict law of the land their presence was not permitted at all. And in Muscovy proper the exclusion was enforced with stern inflexibility. Under Peter the Great a few Jews were admitted into other portions of his dominions, the Czar having declared—so at least popular rumour affirms—that 'he did not fear the presence of any Jews, for his Russians were a match for the craftiest among them.' But during the reign of Elizabeth (a.d. 1545) their residence in Russia was again proscribed. They had contrived to secure the property of certain Siberian exiles, and invested it in foreign countries. Later in the century the policy of the emperors towards the Jews seems to have been to drive them out of the towns into the rural districts, with the idea, so often entertained by one theorist or another, of inducing them to discard commerce for agriculture. In the Ukraine, and there only, apparently, they have adopted that mode of life.[203]

Of the Jews in Poland, which for many ages has been the country in all Europe where the Hebrew race has found the most secure home and the most hospitable treatment, we have not yet spoken. Their history, during the eighteenth century, is mainly the history of religious adventurers and rival sects. It will be better to consider these in a separate chapter.

FOOTNOTES:

[201] J. M. Jost, a German Jew, born a.d. 1793, died 1860, a professor first at Berlin, and afterwards at Frankfort-on-the-Maine. He is the author of the *History of the Israelites*, in nine volumes, published in 1820-28, and of the *History of Judaism*, in three volumes, which appeared later. Up to the time of the appearance of H. Graetz's great work, *The History of the Jews*, Jost's was the most trustworthy authority. 'It is the mature work,' writes Milman, 'of an indefatigable and eminently fair writer. Of course, as a Jew, he presents the doctrines and usages of his race in a favourable light, but he always fully

deserves a respectful and candid hearing' (Milm. *Hist. Jews,* vol. ii. p. 476 n.).

[202] *Israel and the Gentiles* (Da Costa, p. 519), a work I have often consulted with profit.

[203] The readiness of the Jews of the Ukraine to employ themselves in agriculture may be accounted for by the extreme fertility of the soil. In natural productiveness no portion of Europe surpasses, and few can be found to equal it. Wheat, oats, and barley are raised with scarcely any exertion of labour, and the pasture-land is rich and luxuriant. This may account for the singular difference of habits which the Jews of these countries exhibit, as compared with their countrymen everywhere else. It should be added that, as there is little trade and few manufactures, many of them, at all events, must live by agriculture or not at all.

CHAPTER XXXIX
A.D. 1700-1800. THE JEWS IN POLAND:
THE CHASIDIM—FRANK—MENDELSSOHN

From the times of the Maccabees, if not earlier, to those of the impostor Sabbathai Sevi, Rabbinism had prevailed in the Jewish Church. The only opposition had come from the Karaites, of whom we have already spoken, and they were but a small sect, commanding little influence. Eminent Jews, again, such as Solomon Ben Abraham of Montpellier, in the thirteenth century, or Nathanael Tribotti of Rome, or the more renowned Maimonides, might put forward opinions which the Rabbins condemned, proceeding sometimes to the excommunication of the offending writers. But either the latter submitted, or modified their opinions, or their judges reconsidered their decisions; and Rabbinical theology continued in the main unaltered. But the followers of Sabbathai Sevi formed themselves into a distinct sect, calling themselves Jews indeed, and professing the principal doctrines of the Jewish faith, but differing from it, at the same time, in the most essential particulars.

His followers, as we have seen, were not alienated by his apostasy or undeceived by his death. One prophet rose after another, who formed his own theological system, resembling Sabbathaism in its general outline, but having peculiar and distinctive features of its own. Most of these secured, during their lifetime, at all events, a large and enthusiastic following, while, in some instances, their teaching was adopted as a rule of faith long after they had passed away from earth. Among these prophets two of the most remarkable were Malach and Hajun. These men were two Rabbins belonging, the one to a Polish, the other to a German, synagogue, who, a.d. 1700, had made a pilgrimage to Jerusalem, there to announce the immediate coming of the Messiah. Most of their companions died of want or fatigue on the journey; and nearly all the survivors, following the example of Sabbathai, went over to Islamism. But the two leaders, and especially Hajun, zealously propagated their opinions, notwithstanding the most determined opposition of the Rabbins of Jerusalem and Constantinople. Among the doctrines preached by Hajun was that of a Trinity of Gods, though the Three were perfect in their unity. This dogma—very nearly coinciding, if not identical, with the Catholic doctrine of the Trinity—he professed to find in the Book of Zohar.[204]

It is scarcely necessary to add that such teaching provoked the animosity of the Rabbins to the utmost. In a.d. 1722 Hajun and his followers were publicly excommunicated by all the synagogues, and his influence in the East was almost entirely destroyed. In Central Europe, however, he obtained some support. He ingratiated himself with the Emperor Charles VI. by his denunciation of the Jews, and many congregations in Bohemia and Moravia attached themselves to him. Attempts were made to extend his influence into Holland, Hungary, and other European countries, but with little success. A similar movement was initiated shortly afterwards by Moses Luzzato; who, in concert with a physician named Jethukiel, collected a congregation at Wilna. He was excommunicated by the Rabbins, and repeatedly obliged to retract his statements. He led a wandering, unsettled life, and at last travelled to Jerusalem, where he ended his days in 1747.

Another and more important sect, appearing at least to derive its origin from Sabbathaism, is that of the Chasidim, which established itself chiefly in Poland, Galicia, and Russia. This is, according to a well-known writer of the present day, the religion of nearly all the Jews in Galicia, Hungary, Southern Russia, and Wallachia. Its founder was one Israel Baal Schem, who first appeared in Podolia in 1740. He claimed to be the representative of God on earth, and as such, his commands were to be obeyed with implicit submission. His early history is full of fable, wild, extravagant tales being told of it, which are unworthy of repetition. The orthodox Rabbins say he was a man of mean rank and extraction, possessed of no real ability, and who affected sanctity and mystery in order to impress his followers. A certain supernatural power was invariably claimed by the students of Cabbalism, but those assumed by Israel had apparently no limit. He could absolve from all sin; he could cure all diseases by his simple command; he could work the most stupendous miracles; he was endowed with all knowledge, not only of the past, but of the future also. The main drift of his teaching, which entirely rejected the Talmud as a Rabbinical tradition, was the necessity of learning, by continual contemplation and self-mortification, the true nature of God, and also of entire submission to the Tzaddikhim, or priesthood. We are told by Dr. M'Caul that they are in the habit of spending every Sabbath with their Tzaddik, coming in for the purpose from many miles round, bringing with them provisions for the meals of the day, as well as presents for the Tzaddik. They consult him in all difficulties, accepting his replies as inspired by Heaven; arrange their private affairs, and compose their quarrels at his bidding. At Israel Baal Schem's death, his disciples insist that he was taken up to heaven, there to dwell with the holy angels, and make effectual intercession with Almighty God in behalf of every Jew who brings up his children in accordance with the teaching of Chasidism, and obeys the Tzaddik. He was succeeded in his authority by his three grandsons, who were his chief disciples. But this of necessity broke up the community into three distinct bodies, and further divisions have since taken place, though the various synagogues of Chasidists spread over the countries of Eastern Europe are on the whole at unity with one another.

A few years later another strange development of Cabbalistic Sabbathaism made its appearance, under the name of Zoharism. Jacob Frank, its founder, is said to have been born in Poland, *circ.* a.d. 1722. In his youth he was a distiller of brandy, and he first appeared as a religious teacher in Turkey, a.d. 1760. He was then approaching his fortieth year. He followed the Chasidists in his attacks on the Talmud and his devotion to the Book of Zohar. Such fierce dissensions ensued that the Polish Government,—for it was in Poland that he first put forth his theological dogmas,—found it necessary to interfere. But Frank found a protector in the Bishop of Kaminiek, who perceived, or thought he perceived, in Frank's system the elements of Catholic Christianity. Frank himself encouraged this by submitting to Christian baptism, and publicly burning the Talmud. He also declared his belief that God had appeared in human form for the expiation of man's transgression, and that He will hereafter appear again, also in human form, for the final deliverance from the power of evil. This sounded orthodox enough; but Frank was careful not to say in whose person God had thus appeared on earth, and whether, in fact, he accepted Jesus Christ, or Sabbathai Sevi, as the Messiah.

But neither the Jews nor the Christians were content to leave matters in this condition. The Rabbins, who regarded Frank with a mixture of alarm and dislike, denounced him to the Polish Government as an apostate to their community (and so legally liable to their censure), and to the papal nuncio as an heretical Christian. Neither of the parties appealed to were disposed to overlook the accusation; and the Zoharites found themselves on the brink of a twofold persecution. Frank himself was thrown into prison, and his followers were scattered in all directions, most of them endeavouring to seek a refuge in Turkey. On their way, while passing through Moldavia, they received harsh usage from both the authorities and the populace. Those that remained behind were obliged to profess Christianity. Frank himself remained in prison, until the fortress in which he was confined was captured, in 1777, by the Russians, who set him at liberty. He then travelled through Poland, Moravia, and Bohemia, everywhere levying large sums on the synagogues which still continued to support him, until he reached Vienna, where he resided for several years, under the protection of Maria

Theresa. From thence he journeyed to Brunn, in Moravia, and finally established himself at Offenbach, in Hesse, where he resided until his death, in 1791.

A strange mystery attended his daily life, upon which no light has ever been thrown. He was apparently without pecuniary resources, yet he lived for many years—ten or twelve at the least—in a style which could only have been maintained by the most lavish expenditure. He had a retinue which might have vied with that of an Eastern prince, of several hundred beautiful Jewish boys and girls; carts, said to contain gold and silver, were continually brought to his place of residence; when he went to perform his devotions, he was conveyed in a chariot drawn by the finest horses that could be procured, and a guard of ten or twelve Uhlans, wearing a splendid uniform of green, scarlet, and gold, rode on either side of it. The service was performed with a great display of magnificence, accompanied by various strange ceremonies, the meaning of which has never been explained. When he died, as he did some three years after his settlement at Offenbach, he was buried with the utmost pomp and splendour, as many as eight hundred persons attending his funeral; and a costly cross was set up over his grave. But the secret of his unbounded riches was interred with him. His family, it was found, had been left entirely destitute. They appealed to his followers, who had shown such devotion, but wholly in vain; and they relapsed into absolute beggary. Such of his followers as survived him joined the Roman Catholic Church of Poland. It is believed, however, that they still cherish in secret some of their founder's peculiar tenets.

Nearly about the same time another Jew appeared, very different in character and opinions from Jacob Frank, but destined to exercise a far wider and more permanent influence. Moses Mendelssohn was born of humble parents in Dessau, a.d. 1729. His thirst for learning showed itself from his childhood, and his early application to study is said to have permanently injured his health. At the age of thirteen he followed his favourite teacher, Rabbi Frankels, to Berlin, where, after many years of labour, he obtained a tutorship in the family of Herr Bernhardt, a silk manufacturer. Soon after he formed an acquaintance with the philosopher Lessing,[205] and became known in the literary world by the publication of his philosophical works, and especially of *Phædon, or the Immortality of the Soul,* in imitation of Plato. Other works followed, which increased his celebrity. Having obtained the prize of the Berlin Academy for an essay on the Evidence of Metaphysical Science, he was elected a member of that society; but Frederick the Great struck his name off the list, considering that a Jew was not worthy to belong to so august a body. His writings nevertheless continued to attract popular admiration; and the entire emancipation from the fetters of Rabbinism which they displayed encouraged many of his friends to hope that he was already a Christian in principle, and was on the high road to adopting it as his profession. The celebrated Lavater addressed a letter to him, urgently entreating him to take this step. But Mendelssohn courteously but firmly refused, remaining nominally a member of the Jewish synagogue to the day of his death, though he absolutely refused to allow his spiritual pastors to impose any restrictions on his private judgment. It seems to have been his principle to minimize the differences between Christianity and Judaism, and, while remaining a Jew in name, to be a Christian in spirit.

Mendelssohn's name is greatly honoured and admired, but it may be gravely questioned whether the course he pursued was either defensible in itself or beneficial in its results. None of his followers have been able to maintain the position he took up. Some have adopted the genuine faith of Christ, some have renounced distinctive religion altogether. It was remarkable that all Mendelssohn's descendants, including the famous Mendelssohn-Bartholdy, the composer, became Christians. So did Louis Borne, and Neander, the historian and the renowned poet, Heinrich Heine.

We must not pass over Mendelssohn's three celebrated friends— Wessely, the father of modern Hebrew poetry, David Friedlander, the founder of the Jews' Free School at Berlin, and Isaac Euchel, the translator of the Jewish prayer-book. These men, though less distinguished than their great contemporary, have exercised so large an influence on their countrymen and co-religionists that they may be said to have almost entirely changed the tone of Jewish thought and feeling.[206] The synagogue service has also undergone considerable alteration. The prayers and sacred poems have been abridged, and preaching very generally introduced. Even the use of organs is not unusual. Indeed, the old stereotyped service seems to have been exchanged for a ritual according in minor matters with the sentiments and inclination of each congregation.

In Russia, during this century, the condition of the Jews seems to have varied according to the caprices alike of the rulers and the people. They were admitted within the Muscovite kingdom by Peter the Great; but in the reign of Elizabeth, a.d. 1745, their residence was again forbidden, on the ground that they had been maintaining a treasonable correspondence with some Siberian exiles. The expulsion could not have been general, since only a few years later, in 1753, the old charge of sacrificing children was again alleged against them; an appeal was made to the reigning pope, Benedict XIV., and his successor (Clement XIII.) undertook to make an investigation. He accordingly commissioned Count Bruhl to inquire into the matter, adding, to his honour, that he was to disregard all hearsay evidence, and be satisfied with nothing short of proof. It needs not to add that he did not obtain that. But the popular fury rose to such a height that an imperial ukase was found necessary to control it. The same charge has been repeated since, with the same total absence of evidence, even in our time.

FOOTNOTES:

[204] 'There be Three Lights in God: the Ancient Light, the Pure Light, the Purified Light. These three make one God.' For Book of Zohar, see Appendix.

[205] Nathan the Jew, the hero of Lessing's famous play, *Nathan der Weiss*, was designed as a portrait of Mendelssohn.

[206] There were other distinguished men belonging to this age, which, indeed, was unusually rife in literary talent. Joel Lowe, professor at Breslau; Herr Homberg, superintendent of Jewish education in Galicia; Aaron Wolfsohn, also professor at Breslau; and Solomon Maimon, author of several philosophical works and his own autobiography.

CHAPTER XL
A.D. 1700-1800. THE JEWS IN ENGLAND

During this century no marked change of any kind took place in the position of the English Jews, though their affairs several times came before the notice of the legislature. They had obtained under the Stuarts liberty to carry on their public worship, to practise all trades and professions, and hold all property, except such as was not permitted to aliens. None of these privileges were withdrawn or modified during the eighteenth century. On the other hand, the Jews were not naturalized, could not possess land, could not hold any public office of whatsoever kind—were not, in any real sense, English citizens. Yet it was evident they regarded themselves as permanent settlers in the country. They began to build synagogues, and to establish schools, hospitals, and other charitable foundations for the benefit of their community. It should be noted that, as in Holland, so in England also, there were two classes of Jews—the German and Polish (called the Ashkenazim), and the Spanish and Portuguese (the Sephardim).[207] These agree in their religious opinions, but in other matters differ considerably from each other, and it is said that intermarriages between them were for a long time rare. The last-named were the first to erect a synagogue, which was opened in 1662, in King Street, Aldgate. In 1676, a larger synagogue had to be provided, and a third was built three years later. This stands in Bevis Marks, and remains to this day, but little changed in appearance. In 1703 the Jews' Hospital was opened, which now stands in Mile End Road. In 1730 a girls' school was built by Isaac da Costa, and called after his name; and in 1735 another school for general education was set up and endowed by Ruez Lamego.

The German and Polish Jews did not settle in England for a generation later. They were, on the whole, inferior in respect of culture and education, as well as less wealthy, than their Spanish brethren. They provided themselves with a place of worship about the beginning of the last century. It was enlarged in 1722. The present Hamburg synagogue was erected in 1726; and the Great Synagogue, in Duke Street, in 1763.

The first legislation of the century respecting the Jews was in 1703, when an Act was carried obliging the Jews to make provision for any members of their family who might become converts to Christianity. This was passed in consequence of the action of a wealthy Jew, whose daughter had been baptized; immediately after which he turned her out of doors in a state of entire destitution. Not long afterwards, the question of their naturalization began for the first time to be agitated. A proposal was made to the Treasurer Godolphin, in Queen Anne's time, to purchase the town of Brentford for their occupation, the purchase carrying with it the full rights of citizenship. Godolphin was urged by influential persons to accept it. But he foresaw the opposition which both the merchants and the clergy would offer to it, and declined the proposal. A few years afterwards a pamphlet was issued by the notorious John Toland,[208] who has very generally been branded as an infidel, but who appears to have been really guilty of nothing worse than eccentricity. He urged the wisdom and justice of naturalizing the Jews. But John Toland, one of whose works had been ordered to be burnt by the public hangman, was not a very likely person to be listened to on such a subject. It appears to have drawn forth a pamphlet, written in 1715, deprecating in strong language the proposed naturalization. It is curious to read this pamphlet, which may be seen at the British Museum. The writer repeats with unabated acrimony the charges which had been made for centuries against the Jews, but which the English people had now happily ceased to act upon. It says the reasons why Edward I. expelled them from England were, first, their crucifying and torturing Christian children; secondly, their betraying the secrets of the State to foreign enemies; thirdly, their tampering with and debasing the coinage; fourthly, the hatred which they bore to Christian men; and, lastly, their extortionate usuries. Of these, the first two could hardly be expected to obtain any credit, and must have been repeated merely for form's sake, like the preamble of a deed. The fourth, too, almost all men at that day would reject as absurd in itself; because, if the Jews really entertained this bitter hate against Englishmen, why should they be so anxious to dwell among them? The third and fifth undoubtedly have some truth, though the charge of debasing the coinage was never satisfactorily proved, and at all events could not reasonably be charged on the Jews of the eighteenth century. With the last we have more than once dealt in this history. The idea, again, that the Jews are the enemies of Heaven, and that showing favour to them is disloyalty to Almighty God, already belonged only to the past. The writer's real ground for objecting is, no doubt, the injury supposed to be done to English trade by the competition of the Jews, whose presence in England he is anxious to prove does not increase the wealth of the community. No Naturalization Bill was introduced, but in 1723 another step was taken towards improving their condition. It was then enacted that when any one of His Majesty's subjects professing the Jewish religion shall present himself to take the customary oath of abjuration of the Pretender's supposed rights in England, he shall be permitted to omit the words 'On the true faith of a Christian.' This is the first time that any regard for a Jew's conscience or feelings was manifested in any public document. In 1740 another Act of Parliament conceded to foreign Jews who had served for two years on board a British man-of-war the privilege of British citizenship.

In 1753 Mr. Pelham, at that time Premier, brought forward his famous Act for the naturalization of the Jews. One reason for it is said to have been the loyal services rendered by the Jews to the Crown during the attempt of Charles Edward, in 1745, to regain the throne.[209] The Bill was introduced into the House of Lords early in the session, and passed without opposition,[210] almost without remark. It provided for the naturalization of all Jews who had resided in England for three years consecutively. But it should be noted that it did not permit them to hold any public offices, not even of the most petty character. They could not even be excisemen or custom-house officers. Nevertheless, notwithstanding the extreme moderation of the Bill, when it was brought into the Commons, an angry debate ensued. Some members declared that to admit Jews to the privilege of citizenship was an insult to the Christian faith. The inspired Word, it was said, had declared that they should be scattered over the face of the earth, having nowhere any fixed abode; to give them a permanent home, therefore, was to fly in the face of God and of prophecy. It would deluge the kingdom with Jew usurers, brokers, and beggars. The Jews would buy up advowsons, and so ruin the Church! Pelham answered, that the fears expressed were idle and chimerical, that the Jews were too few and uninfluential to work any of the mischief that had been predicted; and, as they could not take any part in our religious services, or even enter our churches, it was impossible they could injure the Church. As for any supposed opposition to the will of God, if there had been any such Divine decree as was represented, it would be impossible for man to overthrow or even to modify it. The Bill passed by a majority of ninety-five, only sixteen being found to vote against it. But the Bill, though accepted by Parliament, excited out of doors a perfect storm of indignation. The peers, and especially the bishops,[211] were pursued by mobs with insult and rancour. The common people filled the streets with cries of 'No Jews—no wooden shoes!' 'The wooden shoes' were typical of the French peasants, who ordinarily wore them. The popular *brocard* 'No wooden shoes' thus meant 'Nothing French.' There was no kind of connection between the Jews and the French, but the rhyme between 'Jews' and 'shoes' hit the popular fancy, and so the two cries were combined in one.

The members of the House of Commons were threatened with the loss of their seats; and, as Parliament was near its last session, this was no idle menace. As the autumn advanced, the agitation increased. A clergyman named Tucker, who had written a pamphlet in defence of the measure, was attacked and maltreated by the mob. The Bishop of Norwich, Thomas Gooch, also an advocate of the measure, when he went down to his diocese on his confirmation circuit, was everywhere insulted. At Ipswich the boys whom he was about to confirm shouted out to him that they wished to be circumcised; and on the door of one of the churches a paper was found, announcing that the bishop would confirm the Jews on the Saturday, and the Christians on the Sunday next ensuing.

It was not by the mob only that these clamours were raised. The Lord Mayor and Corporation of London, actuated, it is to be feared, by commercial jealousy, publicly denounced the measure as an inroad on the Constitution and an insult to the Christian religion, and the country clergy everywhere preached the same from their pulpits.

The ministry found that they could not withstand the popular fury. On the very first day of the ensuing session, immediately after the Peers had agreed to the usual address to the Crown, the Duke of Newcastle made an harangue, declaring that disaffected persons had made use of the Act passed last session in favour of the Jews to raise discontent among His Majesty's subjects. As the Act itself was of little importance, it had better be repealed. As little opposition was offered to this proposal as to the original Bill. Some few did indeed protest against this concession to mob clamour; amongst them the Bishop of St. Asaph and Lord Temple. But in the Lower House both parties seemed to vie with each other in expressing their aversion to this unfortunate measure.

Even this ready compliance with the popular will did not allay the ferment that had been excited. There was, it appeared, an Act in existence, by virtue of which any Jew who had resided for seven years in any of His Majesty's American plantations might become a free denizen of Great Britain. It was discovered that this was fraught with almost as much danger to the interests of the English people as the obnoxious measure which had just been removed from the statute book. A member of the Lower House moved that a list of the Jews who had availed themselves of the benefit of this Act since 1740 should be laid on the table for the perusal of the members of the House. It was found that, as claiming the privilege in question was attended by a good deal of expense and trouble, very few Jews had availed themselves of it. Nevertheless, as the *possibility* still remained that Jews in great numbers would at some future time take advantage of the Act in question, and so deluge England with Jews, whose presence would be in the highest degree prejudicial to the interests and even the safety of Great Britain, Lord Harley asked for leave to bring in a Bill to strike out of the Act its obnoxious clauses. But at this point Government refused to concede any further to out-door clamour. Lord Harley's motion was seconded by Sir James Dashwood, and supported by other influential persons. But Mr. Pitt made one of his great speeches against it, and it was rejected by a decisive majority. The whole affair is a curious instance of how easily the English people may be stirred up to loud and clamorous indignation upon the most trivial subjects, in which neither their safety nor their convenience are in any way concerned;[212] though they cannot, like their Continental neighbours, be induced to proceed to acts of violence, unless where some real danger threatens them or some important interest is at stake.

During the remainder of the century, and indeed for a large part of that which followed, no new attempt was made to accomplish the naturalization of the Jews. It was probably felt by their friends that the angry and unreasonable prejudice which had been roused by the proposed measure of 1753 would in all likelihood break out as virulent as ever,[213] if a similar Bill should be brought into Parliament. It is also a singular fact that many of the Jews themselves were not anxious for the measure to pass, as they feared that the conversion of many of their communion to the Christian faith might follow from it.

But there were not wanting signs that the feeling towards the Jews was gradually growing more considerate and kindly. In 1781, when the island of St. Eustatia was captured by Rodney, a complaint was made in Parliament that undue severity had been shown the Jews in seizing their property, and transporting them from the island. General Vaughan, who commanded the land forces, represented that he had shown the Jews the greatest consideration, had caused their persons to be respected, and, on finding that their property had been seized by mistake, had immediately ordered it to be restored to them. No more had been done for them than justice required; but the tone of both parties, when speaking of the Jews, was strikingly different from what it probably would have been had the occurrence taken place some generations earlier.

Towards the close of the century, a body known as the Board of Deputies was formed, which gave the Jews the means of expressing in an official manner the wants and sentiments of the Jewish residents in Great Britain. It was originally appointed for the purpose of conveying to George III. the congratulations of the Jews in England on his accession to the throne. Once established, it renewed its meeting when occasion required, and has frequently played an important part in Jewish affairs.

FOOTNOTES:

[207] Ashkenaz, the son of Gomer (Gen. x. 3), is traditionally reported to have settled in Germany. Zarephath and Sephared (Obad. 20) in France and Spain. Hence the German and Spanish Jews have been styled Ashkenazim and Sephardim. These being at one time the principal countries in which the European Jews were found, have caused the whole of the nation to be classed under one head or the other.

[208] John Toland, as he was called, though his true baptismal names were James Julius, was born in Londonderry in 1669. His parents were Roman Catholics, but he seems early to have rejected Romish teaching. He studied successively at Glasgow, Leyden, and Oxford. At the last-named university he seems to have obtained the reputation of a freethinker; and his book, *Christianity not Mysterious*, excited a ferment which there is little or nothing to justify. It was condemned by the Irish Parliament, and burnt by the hangman. Leland ranks him among Deistical writers; but he hardly seems to deserve, and is certainly not worth, Leland's censures.

[209] The Jews had given the Government valuable help. They lent a large sum on very liberal terms, and agreed to take the Government paper as long as gold continued to be scarce. Two Jews fitted out vessels at their own cost, which they placed at the service of the king. Great numbers of Jews also enrolled themselves in the volunteer troops hastily raised by the ministry.

[210] Lord Lyttelton, the author of the *Life of Henry II.*, is said to have declared on this occasion that 'the man who hated another because he was not a Christian, was no Christian himself'—a sentiment worthy of him.

[211] It is a singular fact that, although the bishops had nothing to do with the promotion of this Bill, the principal odium of it was cast upon them. It was held that they were bound in conscience to prevent its passing, or at all events to do their best to prevent it. William Romaine affirmed, in a pamphlet which attracted much attention, that 'the set of bishops then on the bench were the only ones from the time of Christ who would have countenanced so anti-Christian a

measure.' The general charge made against bishops is that of intolerance. It is curious to observe that, if they ever are in advance of the laity in tolerance, it is at once made the subject of bitter reproach to them.

[212] It is a most curious illustration of this that, up to the middle of the present century, although all bequests made by Jews to their countrymen for charitable purposes, such as building hospitals, endowing almshouses, etc., were held valid, and would be enforced, if necessary, by the Court of Chancery, any provision for the education of their children in their own faith was accounted void. A bequest made about the middle of the century, by a Jew named De Pass, of £1,200 for the purpose of building a college for Jews, was similarly declared void by the Law Courts, because it tended to propagate a false belief, and the money was given to the Foundling Hospital.

[213] During the No Popery riots of 1780, the Jews in Houndsditch, fearing that the violence of the mob would be attracted to them, as it had so often been on occasions of popular tumult, wrote up each on his door front: 'This is the house of a true Protestant.' The father of Grimaldi, the clown, is said to have exercised a still more comprehensive caution, and to have inscribed on *his* door, not 'No Popery,' but 'No Religion.' Lord George Gordon, the leader of the riots, consummated his erratic career by professing the Jewish faith, in which he died.

CHAPTER XLI
A.D. 1800-1885. THE JEWS IN
ENGLAND—*continued*

It does not surprise us, as was remarked in the last chapter, that no step was taken to amend the position of the Jews during the latter half of the eighteenth or the first quarter of the nineteenth century. For many years after the struggle of 1753 its memory was fresh in men's minds; and to have attempted its renewal would only have called forth a more bitter expression of hostility. Then the struggle with America, the horrors of the French Revolution, the excitement of Napoleon's wars, the trade riots and domestic disturbances of the later years of the Regency engrossed men's minds, and they had neither leisure nor inclination to attend to the grievances of the Jews. Even when, in George the Fourth's reign, questions of internal policy again became the topic of the day, the disabilities of the Roman Catholics, a numerous and influential portion of the nation, naturally took precedence of those of the Jews. But when these had been removed, and the Test and Corporation Act had, in 1829, been repealed, the Board of Deputies, already referred to, felt that their opportunity had arrived. They applied to the leading statesmen of the day, and among others to the Duke of Wellington, pointing out that, as he had recently carried through Parliament a Bill for the relief of the Roman Catholics, he was in consistency bound to do the like for the relief of the Jews. But the duke answered that such an attempt would raise so angry an outcry as to render the success of the measure hopeless.

Nevertheless, something was done. The first step was taken in 1828, when the restrictions were removed which had been imposed on the admission of the Jews to the Stock Exchange. Up to that time only twelve Jewish brokers had been allowed there, and the privilege of entry had to be purchased by the payment of a large sum to the Lord Mayor.[214] This was now abolished; and in 1830 Mr. Robert Grant, afterwards Lord Advocate in the Grey Ministry, introduced into the House of Commons a Bill for the removal of Jewish Disabilities. It was rejected by the large majority of 163. The Reformed House of Commons passed it three years afterwards, but it was thrown out in the House of Lords.

Still the cause of the Jews progressed. In 1830 an Act was passed, legalizing Jewish marriages, which the law, up to that time, had not recognised. In 1832 they were admitted to the franchise, and became free of the City. They were now allowed to open shops there, which they had hitherto been prohibited from doing. In 1833 a Jew, Mr. Goldsmid, was admitted as a barrister by the Society of Lincoln's Inn. In 1835 Mr. Salomons, also a Jew, was made Sheriff of Middlesex. In 1837 Mr. Montefiore was knighted by the Queen; and in 1844 the Jews were declared eligible to all municipal offices. Mr. Salomons was made an Alderman in 1847, and Lord Mayor in 1856.

About this time a movement was set on foot in London for the reformation of the Jewish Church there. It is stated that during the first half of the present century the services in the synagogues were ill-conducted and poorly attended. Attempts were made by some zealous members of the community to bring about an improvement, but for a long time with little success, until, in 1841, matters came to a crisis. The reformers, among whom Sir Isaac Goldsmid was conspicuous, withdrew from their brethren, and built what was called the Reformed Synagogue, now situated in Upper Berkeley Street. The object of the seceders was mainly to improve the existing liturgy, partly by shortening it, partly by the removal of certain expressions in the prayers which do not harmonize with the feelings of educated Jews in the present day.[215] A good deal of angry feeling was called forth on the occasion, and the excommunications of the seceders were freely pronounced. After a few years, however, this began to subside, and has now, we are told, vanished altogether. Both the Sephardim and Ashkenazim, indeed, have made considerable alteration in their liturgies in the course of the present century.

In 1847 an important step was taken by the leaders of the Jewish emancipationists. At the general election in that year Baron Lionel Rothschild offered himself as a candidate for the city of London, and was returned. When the session of 1849 opened, Lord John Russell, then Premier, brought in a Bill to omit from the Parliamentary oath the words, 'on the true faith of a Christian,' which rendered it impossible for a Jew to take it. The Bill was carried by a majority of 66. It was then introduced into the House of Lords by the Earl of Carlisle, who urged that the Jews were now the only persons excluded from Parliament on account of their religious opinions. As uniformity of belief on religious subjects had ceased to be required as the condition of admission to the legislature, it was obviously unjust to exclude Jews on that ground. The Bill was opposed by the Archbishop of Canterbury, who argued that the measure was inconsistent with the national profession of Christianity; also by the Bishop of Exeter, who declared it to be a breach of the contract made between the sovereign and the nation—that 'the Crown should maintain the laws of God, and the true profession of the Gospel.' On the other side, Archbishop Whately argued that the spirit of Christianity forbids us to require the imposition of civil penalties on those who differ from it. On a division the Bill was lost by a majority of 25.

An attempt of a different character was now made to obtain the object desired. On the 26th of July, 1850, Baron Rothschild presented himself before the Speaker to take the necessary oath; and when the Clerk presented the New Testament, he said, 'I desire to be sworn on the Old Testament.' Sir R. Inglis rose to oppose this suggestion; the baron was ordered to withdraw, and a long debate ensued. The opinion of the law officers of the Crown having been taken, the House resolved that Baron Rothschild could not take the oath, except in the ordinary manner prescribed by the law. It was agreed, however, that another Bill should be introduced for the relief of the Jews in the ensuing session.

This was accordingly done. The Bill was brought in and carried, though by a reduced majority, and was then sent up to the Lords, by whom it was, as before, thrown out. Its rejection was followed by a second attempt, similar to that of Baron Rothschild in the preceding year. Alderman Salomons, who had been returned for the borough of Greenwich, presented himself at the table, and demanded to be sworn on the Old Testament. He was ordered to withdraw, but refused to do so, until given into the custody of the Serjeant-at-Arms. He also voted in two or three divisions, although he had not taken the oath. The House declared this procedure to be illegal, and an action was brought against Alderman Salomons in the Court of Exchequer to recover of him the penalty of £500, which he was said to have incurred by voting in the House of Commons without having previously taken the oath. Judgment was given for the plaintiff. Mr. Salomons appealed, and the case was again heard before six of the judges, but they confirmed the decision of the previous court.

From that time until 1858 Bills were repeatedly brought into the Lower House, and passed by majorities, sometimes larger and sometimes smaller, until the year above named, when, under a Conservative Government, the Commons admitted the Jews by a resolution setting aside the standing order of the House, and Baron Rothschild took his seat as the first Jewish member. In 1860 a Bill was passed through both Houses, allowing the Jews to omit from the Parliamentary oath the words, 'on the true faith of a Christian.' To complete the history of Jewish emancipation, it should here be added that in 1873 Sir George Jessel was made Master of the Rolls, being the first Jew admitted to the English Bench; and in 1885 Sir N. Rothschild was created a peer, the first who has entered the English House of Lords. No Jew has as yet been a Cabinet Minister; but it is obvious that, whenever it shall serve the interest of the party which has for the time a predominance in the country to make a Jew Lord Chancellor, or one of the Secretaries of State, or even Premier, there will be no legal obstacle, and probably no opposition offered to such a measure. The struggle, in fact, is over. The Jews are fully emancipated.

The history of this protracted strife is full of interest to the student of Jewish history, because it illustrates in the most forcible manner the difference of opinion in men's minds respecting the Jews, which has existed from the earliest ages of the Church—which, indeed, still exists, notwithstanding the great change in their condition which this present century has brought about. Many sincere Christians still think that the nation, in admitting Jews to the legislature, has been guilty of a breach of its duty in the sight of God. There is, first of all, the belief that the Jews are a people lying under the curse of God, and that to show any favour to them is to rebel against this decree. We have seen what revolting barbarities this idea led to during the Dark and Middle Ages. Its nineteenth-century form—of standing aloof, and withholding civil rights from them—is less shocking in its results, but equally false in principle. God has doubtless His own purposes towards them, and they are a standing miracle, an enduring evidence of the truth of His prophetic word. But He has not commanded us to be the instruments of what we may suppose to be His pleasure, and can do His work without our help. Every faithful follower of St. Paul will regard the Jews in the same light in which he regards them.[216] Every sincere believer in the Lord will echo the same prayer[217] that He offered for them. Again, there are those who, though they would repudiate the notion above suggested, still think, with Archbishop Sumner, that the admission of the Jew to the legislature is a repudiation of our national Christianity; or, with Bishop Philpotts, that it is a breach of the sovereign's coronation oath. If this were so, no faithful believer, no loyal citizen could uphold the measure. But let us consider what this 'admission to the legislature' really amounts to. A Jew who enters Parliament cannot, in consequence of his entry, himself make or alter laws. He has only one voice out of a thousand in any legislative enactment. It will be said that he ought not to have any voice at all. But if so, he must not have the elective suffrage; or he may help to return a member who represents his opinions. Nay, even if he has not the suffrage, he may, by the use of his money, his station, his personal character, his tongue as a public speaker, his pen as a writer, exercise a powerful influence in the settlement of public affairs, which is, in fact, legislation. The only mode of preventing him from doing this would be to do as our forefathers did in England, as Torquemada did in Spain—to forbid him to dwell in the land at all. They were at least consistent, and could be so in no other way.

Again, does the sovereign, by giving the royal assent to a Bill for the removal of Jewish disabilities, violate the undertaking of the coronation oath, 'to maintain the laws of God, and the true profession of the Gospel'? By the 'laws of God' we must, I presume, understand 'the *commandments* of God' to be meant. The phrase occurs continually in Scripture in that, and no other, sense. But how is the maintenance of these impaired by the admission to the legislature of the Jew, who acknowledges these commandments as religiously as does the Christian? Again, there is 'the true profession of the Gospel'—that is, I conclude, the profession of the Gospel, untainted by heresy or falsehood. But the Jew would have no power of tainting this, though he *were* to become a member of Parliament. Parliament does not determine theological controversies, sit in judgment on heresies, does not admit candidates for orders, does not ordain or consecrate. If the Jew were to be allowed, through his election to the House of Commons, to meddle with any of these things, that would, no doubt, be a very different matter, which all loyal Churchmen would resist to the utmost. But notoriously the Jewish member of Parliament neither possesses nor desires anything of the kind.[218]

There is, in truth, a confusion in some men's minds between 'God's laws' and Christian dogmas, which misleads them. As Head of the State, the sovereign upholds the 'laws of God'—of public morality, that is to say— which are rightly so called, because they are primarily of God's ordering. These, all men, whatever be their distinctive creed, are bound to support. As the Head of the Church, again, the sovereign maintains Christian dogmas through the ministrations of those who hold offices in that Church, and takes cognisance of denials and perversions of the Faith. To these offices there never has been any proposal to admit the Jews, nor is there the least likelihood that such ever will be made.

FOOTNOTES:

[214] Sir Moses Montefiore paid £1,200 for his admission to the Stock Exchange.

[215] In the twelfth prayer, used by the Jews for many centuries, in their public worship, occurred the words: 'Let there be no hope for those who apostatize from the true religion, and let heretics, however so many they be, perish in a moment. And let the kingdom of pride (the Roman empire) be speedily rooted out and broken in our days.' In

the liturgy of the Ashkenazim this prayer (which tradition attributes to Gamaliel) now stands thus: 'Let the slanderers have no hope, all the wicked be annihilated speedily, and all tyrants be cut off quickly.' In that of the Sephardim the prayer runs: 'Let slanderers have no hope, and let all presumptuous apostates perish in a moment. May Thine enemies and those that hate Thee be suddenly cut off, and all those that act wickedly be suddenly consumed, broken, and rooted out; and humble Thou them speedily in our days.' — Horne's *Introduction*, iii. 474.

[216] Romans x. 1.

[217] Luke xxiii. 34.

[218] Sir G. Jessel would not present to a living, which was in his patronage as Master of the Rolls, on the very grounds here alleged — that he had nothing to do, and ought to have nothing to do, with the Christian Church. No doubt, in the present anomalous state of things, questions relative to the Church might be brought before Parliament with which no Jew could with any propriety interfere. But if he is to be excluded on that ground, then all but genuine members of the Church ought to be excluded also.

CHAPTER XLII
A.D. 1800-1885. THE JEWS IN FRANCE, ITALY, AND GERMANY

We hear no more of the Jews in France, after the relief granted them by the Republican Government, until 1806; when Napoleon, who by his victory at Austerlitz had obtained almost undisputed supremacy in Europe, was arranging his schemes for carrying out that darling dream of his imagination, the Continental system. Few men were keener or more far-sighted than Napoleon. It cannot be doubted that he saw the great value which the cordial co-operation of the Jews would be to him, if he could only obtain it. Their secret but widespread system of mutual intercommunication,[219] their wealth, their intelligence, their perfect mastery of the principles of commerce, would greatly facilitate the designs he contemplated. It is probable that even then he meditated the resuscitation of the Kingdom of Poland, as a formidable opponent to Russia; and the vast number of Jews to be found in those countries rendered their goodwill of the utmost importance to the success of such a scheme. He convoked a meeting of Jews in Paris, which, to gratify their national sentiment, he called a Sanhedrin, and submitted to it twelve questions,[220] mainly relating to their social life and position in France. It had the effect, as he doubtless had anticipated, of drawing forth an assurance of their appreciation of the privileges of French citizenship, and their warm affection for their native land, as they designated France. The Imperial Government professed itself satisfied with the reply. A second Sanhedrin was summoned, at which foreign Jews were invited to attend, and a kind of constitution framed, by which it was hoped that the Jews everywhere throughout Europe would be bound. It was ratified by an imperial edict, and was, on the whole, extremely favourable to them. It took effect in France and all countries to which Napoleon's authority extended, though in some parts, as Alsace, concessions were made to popular prejudice, and the privileges of the Jews curtailed. The effect was soon seen in the purchase of estates by Jewish proprietors, the employment of Jewish capital in manufactures, and the participation of the Jews generally in national schemes of foreign and domestic policy.[221] At the Revolution of 1830 the most complete equality of citizenship was granted them; and since that time there has been no alteration in the laws of France, so far as they are concerned.

In Italy the condition of the Jews has varied very little during this century, though public attention has been once or twice directed to them. In most of the large cities, though they are regarded with a species of tacit dislike, no open wrong is done them. In some, as, for example, Florence, they are treated with strict justice, indeed, it might be said with favour. Their rights are protected, and they are allowed to pursue all trades and professions, except that of the physician. At Rome, on the accession of Pio Nono, among the various liberal measures adopted by him was one in favour of the Jews. At that time they were strictly confined within the precincts of their Ghetto; they were obliged every year to send a deputation of four elders to ask permission to reside during that year at Rome, and they were required to attend periodically to listen to sermons preached for their conversion. All these obligations were annulled by the new pontiff. On the 17th April, 1847, he went in solemn procession to the Ghetto, and ordered the wall of partition between it and the rest of the city to be thrown down. [222] He rescinded the regulations whereby the Jews were compelled to sue for permission to dwell in Rome, and to attend controversial sermons. He even substituted a star for a cross, in an order of merit which he instituted, that he might not offend their feelings. After the Revolution of 1848, however, the old regulations were again enforced.

In the summer of the year 1858 public attention was again drawn to the condition of the Jews in the Papal States. On the 23rd of June in that year Signor Mortara, a cloth merchant of Bologna, received a visit from the police; who, it appeared, had been sent by Padre Felletti, Chief Inquisitor of Bologna. It was night, and Signor Mortara's seven children were all in bed. They were awakened; an inquiry was made as to the names and ages of each; and the parents were then informed that a maid-servant, who had been in their service, had given evidence to the effect that six years before, when one of their children, Edgar by name, had been dangerously ill, she had secretly baptized him. The child was therefore a Christian, and must be given up to the Catholic Church, to be bred up in that faith. The mother screamed and fainted. The father appealed to the Archbishop of Bologna and the Governor, but without effect. The child was forcibly seized by the Carabineers, and sent to Rome.

Signor Mortara followed, and had an interview with Cardinal Antonelli. The line he took does not seem to have been the one which would naturally have suggested itself to an Englishman. He did not represent that, even assuming the girl's statement to be correct, it would be a most monstrous perversion, alike of natural right and Christian doctrine, to suppose that her act could be any sufficient ground for removing a child from the care of its parents, to which the Providence of God had entrusted it. Probably he knew, however, that any such plea would be urged in vain, and that his only chance of success lay in disproving that any such baptism as the servant alleged had ever taken place. He therefore brought forward evidence that the child had not had the dangerous illness which she declared it to have had, and further, that the servant girl's character was so bad that her evidence was of no value. Antonelli was not to be convinced. He did, indeed, so far relent as to allow the parents occasionally to see their son; but the priests continually interfered; and at last, finding probably that they made no progress in reconciling the child to his new life as long as the father and mother had access to him, they conveyed him away altogether.

The story excited a profound sensation throughout Europe. Several of the Great Powers remonstrated with the Vatican, urging that the boy ought to be restored to his parents. Their representations failing, Sir Moses Montefiore, the well-known champion of Jewish rights, undertook a journey to Rome, where he had an interview with Cardinal Antonelli, and asked to be allowed to plead his suit personally with the pope. His efforts were zealously seconded by Mr. Odo Russell, the British Agent, but they proved futile nevertheless. Sir Moses was informed that Pio Nono regarded the affair as one which had been finally settled, and which he declined to reopen. The boy's mother is said to have died of grief. However that may be, it is certain that no more shameful tale of persecution ever disgraced the annals of the Papacy. It is a consolation to know that the establishment of the Italian monarchy brought freedom and civil equality at last to the Jewish people.[223]

In Germany, their history during this century is full of interest, partly on account of the remarkable variations of policy exhibited from time to time in the dealings of the German Government with them, and partly from the conflict of opinion between the ancient Rabbinical schools and what may be called the neology of modern Judaism, which, originating as we have seen with Mendelssohn and his contemporaries, derived afterwards much of its inspiration from Strauss and other kindred writers.

After the fall of Napoleon, when Germany was reconstructed professedly as nearly as possible on its ancient basis, one article of the Federal Act of the Germanic States, promulgated in June, 1815, secured to the Jews the possession of equal rights of citizenship throughout Germany, conditionally only on their compliance with the laws of the State in which they resided. But it is always easier to frame a law than to ensure its observance, and this was especially the case in Germany, which consisted of a great number of federal States, in which there was a great difference of opinion on many subjects, and especially as regarded the status of the Jews. The principle of Jewish equality, social and political, with the Christian inhabitants of every country, did make its way, but very slowly, and several generations passed before it came to be fully acknowledged.

Nor was it only the *vis inertiæ*, so to speak, of public opinion that had to be overcome. In some countries, at all events, there was a positive reaction against the favour which had been shown by Diets and Governments to the Jews. Even as early as 1815, Frankfort, Lubeck, and Bremen made several enactments, revoking the civil privileges which had been granted to the Jews. Commercial jealousy does not seem to have been the main, or at all events the sole, occasion of this change of policy. The Jews were attacked by men of learning and ability, whom we might have expected to be superior to the prejudices they displayed. The faults of their national character were alleged against them—their exclusiveness, their inveterate obstinacy, their greed of gain, and especially the bigotry of their religious belief. This was no doubt offensive to the rationalizing school, which was rising into eminence. Some of the German professors insisted on their being regarded as always and everywhere aliens, who could not be made to amalgamate with any other nation—who might exist in great numbers *in* any land, but would never be of it. The effect of this agitation was, for the time, at all events, to throw back the question of Jewish emancipation. They were excluded from holding magisterial offices, professorships in the Universities, commissions in the army. In some States the question of their expatriation was mooted; it was even carried out at Lubeck, so far as the city itself was concerned. In other places something of the old mediæval outrages were renewed. At Hamburg and other towns the houses of the Jews were pillaged and demolished. It is even said that in some places the old cry of the monk Rodolph, 'Hep, Hep,' was again heard.

The revolutionary outbreak of 1830 in France spread into Germany; but the extreme Liberal party did not now advocate, as before, the entire social and political equality of the Jews with their fellow-citizens. Hatred of dogmatic teaching seems to have overpowered every other consideration; and as the dogmatism of the Jews has always been one of their most marked characteristics, the Rationalist leaders, among whom Bruno Bauer was conspicuous, clamoured for their suppression as a religious community, and the withdrawal of civil rights and privileges from them. The orthodox Jews did not lack able and zealous champions; but, as has been already intimated, it was not from Christians only that they encountered opposition. As some nominal Christians in Germany, and certain others who could hardly claim the title of Christian at all, had dealt with the historical records and theological dogmas of the Gospel, so did nominal Jews deal with those of Judaism. 'In the Synagogue, as in the Church,' says Da Costa,[224] 'everything that was national and Israelitish, all that was supernatural and beyond the reach of unassisted human reason, was furiously attacked and rejected.' It was not merely that novelties were introduced into the ancient Hebrew liturgy and synagogue service, that organs and music were imported, and sermons preached in the German language, and new prayers interpolated, and old prayers excluded, but the fundamental doctrines of their faith were questioned and discredited. One party proposed to abolish the Jewish Sabbath, substituting the Christian Sunday for it. Another openly declared that they looked for and desired no Messiah to come. Another more insidiously averred that they did indeed believe in the future advent of the Hope of Israel, but He was not a Person, but simply the representative of ever-advancing enlightenment and benediction—one who always had been and ever would be coming, but who would never come until the perfection of humanity had been reached. But a theory like this would be more embarrassing to the Jew than its counterpart was to the Christian. Rationalists might declare the Incarnate God to have been a personified myth, an ideal Being, in whose reputed words and acts Christian ideology found embodiment. But there were His words, which no man could have spoken; and there were His acts, which no man could have performed; there were His predictions, which the history of the world since His day had made good, and which nothing but Divine Wisdom could have uttered. The Jews had nothing of this to sustain them, and it cannot surprise us that many among them found no shelter in such a sea of doubt, except in embracing the Christian creed. Hence, in all likelihood, the number of conversions which are reported to have taken place in Germany at this period. Da Costa reports them as having amounted to five thousand in twenty years.

But orthodox Judaism made a resolute stand against the evil. Schools and colleges were established in the great German cities, presided over by learned and zealous teachers: nor is there any lack of distinguished writers and able preachers among them. Among scholars, Raport and Leopold Zunz were pre-eminent;[225] among historians, Geiger and Graetz, the last-named the author of the most copious and learned History of the Jews which has yet appeared. The German Jews have also distinguished themselves in every department of science and literature—in politics, in music, in metaphysics, in medicine, in the *belles lettres*. Their free admission to all public offices, and the full rights of citizenship, dates only from the reconstruction of the German empire; but it is now fully, and we may hope finally, secured.

FOOTNOTES:

[219] Baron Rothschild, by his private agencies, was enabled to inform the British Government of the escape of Napoleon from Elba, and Wellington's victory at Waterloo.

[220] These questions were: 1, 2, 3. Are polygamy, divorce, and intermarriage with Christians allowed by Jewish law? 4, 5, 6. In what light are Frenchmen regarded by Jews, and do the Jews feel themselves bound by the laws of France? 7, 8, 9. In what manner, and by whom, are the Rabbins elected, and what are their powers? 10, 11, 12. Are there any professions forbidden to Jews? Is usury, with their own people, and with strangers, permissible? The Jews answered: that polygamy was forbidden; divorce allowed, if in accordance with the law of the land; intermarriage legal, but not celebrated by any religious rite; that the Jews regarded Frenchmen as their brethren, and acknowledged French law; that any profession was lawful; that the Rabbins were elected according to custom, and had no judicial authority; that legal interest was permitted, but usury forbidden.

[221] In a return made in 1808, scarcely more than a year after Napoleon's edict, it is declared that there were then 80,000 Jews in France, of whom 1,232 were landed proprietors, 250 were manufacturers, and 797 military men, among whom were officers of all ranks, up to field-marshals.

[222] The Ghetto had been thrown open during the French possession of Rome; but in 1815, when Italy returned to its old masters, the former state of things was resumed.

[223] Since the complete consolidation of the Italian kingdom under Victor Emmanuel, the Jews in all parts of Italy have enjoyed the rights of citizenship without any restriction. They are free to live wherever they like, follow any trades or professions, and are entitled to hold the same offices and perform the same duties as all other Italian citizens. The Ghettoes are everywhere abolished—that is, every one who

chooses is permitted to live in them, and no one who does not choose is required to reside there.

[224] *Israel and the Gentiles*, p. 597.

[225] Zunz is the author of a masterly review of Jewish ethics, and two works on the poetry of the mediæval Jews. He also wrote a notice of the celebrated Rashi, and other works.

CHAPTER XLIII
A.D. 1800-1885. THE JEWS IN OTHER EUROPEAN COUNTRIES

In Spain, until quite within the last few years, there was no material change in the condition of the Jews from what it had been during the eighteenth century. In 1808, when Spain fell under the authority of Napoleon, the Inquisition was suppressed. It was revived again when the country returned, in 1814, to the dominion of its native sovereigns, but only to last for a few years, being finally put down by the Cortes in 1820. The old intolerance, however, the iron legislation of Ferdinand and Isabella, still continued virtually in force. Jews, as such, could not reside with any safety in Spain, until—as it has been before observed—quite recently, when the example shown everywhere in civilized Europe has at last had its effect, and the Jews have been permitted to return to a country for which, notwithstanding the persecutions of many generations, they have ever cherished a warm attachment. In 1881, the Spanish Ambassador at Constantinople so far reversed the traditional policy of his country, as to offer a shelter in Spain for some Jewish fugitives from Russia; and in some of the principal Spanish towns Jewish worship is now publicly celebrated.

The same is the case in Portugal. In 1821 the Cortes abolished the Inquisition, restored the ancient rights possessed by the Jews previously to the reign of King Emmanuel, and decreed that Jews might everywhere settle in Portugal.

In Holland and Belgium there is perfect freedom and equality. This dates from 1796, when the French gained possession of the country, and introduced the same regulations which existed among themselves. These were not at first entirely acceptable to the Jewish residents, because, while on the one hand they removed many restrictions hitherto imposed upon them, they also restrained the power of the Rabbins, and required Jews to take part in all public duties and burdens. But the rights of citizenship were found to be a boon more than compensating these drawbacks; and there is now no distinction between them and the native inhabitants of the countries in question.

In Denmark, Sweden, and Norway, the number of Jews is insignificant, and but little attention appears to be paid to them. In Switzerland they were long treated with extreme harshness. French influence, so efficient in other contiguous countries, did very little for them. It is only within the last ten years that religious freedom has been conceded to them by the State.

To pass to a more important country, Austria, the Jews, early in this century, were somewhat severely dealt with. The successors of their great patron and friend, Joseph II., annulled many of the privileges he had granted them. Indeed, for the greater part of the present century they have been subject to what must be regarded as unreasonable restrictions. They were not allowed to rent or purchase land, nor could they remove from one place to another without the special permission of the Government, and a heavy capitation tax was exacted of them. This, however, was reduced in 1848, and twenty years afterwards they obtained from the Government the entire freedom which they now enjoy. Several Jews, we are told, are now members of the legislature.

These regulations have the force of law in Hungary as well as in Austria proper; but neither the Government nor the people accord them the perfect liberty and equality which the law professes to secure. The antipathy to them all over Central Europe is well known. In Hungary, within the last few years, this has been painfully illustrated by the trial at Nyireghyaza, which for many weeks attracted the attention of all Europe. As it illustrates, more forcibly than any comment could do, the true status of the Hungarian Jews, it will be proper to give an outline of the occurrence here.

In March, 1882, a young girl named Esther Solymosi suddenly disappeared. She was discontented with her situation, and had quarrelled with her mistress. A few weeks afterwards, a Jew named Scharf, together with one or two other of his countrymen, was charged with having murdered her, in order to use her blood for ritual purposes. At first, the sole evidence was a Jewish child, five years old, who said that he had seen his father and brother cut the girl's throat, and catch her blood in a basin. The brother, a boy of fourteen, at first denied any knowledge of the transaction, but afterwards retracted the denial. He now said that he had not been present when the deed was done, but he had seen it through the key-hole of the door of the tabernacle. There was no corroborative evidence of his tale, and, in addition to the fact that it was in the teeth of his first evidence, it was proved that it was impossible to see through the key-hole of the door in the way he had described.

Six weeks afterwards a body, which was sworn to be that of Esther Solymosi, was found in the river Theiss. It was dressed in her clothes, and identified by means of a peculiar scar. It was pretended that the body of another person had been dressed in Esther's clothes, in order to frustrate inquiry. But the case broke down, and the Jews were fully acquitted. The verdict was accompanied by an official declaration that the oft-repeated charge made against the Jews, of using Christian blood in their services, is a baseless calumny. But the popular outcry with which the acquittal was received shows how deeply seated the prejudice of the Hungarian people on this subject still is. The inquiry, in fact, revealed a mass of ignorance, prejudice, and uncharity which would have been bad enough in the twelfth century, but which in the nineteenth is almost incredible. The lower classes, indeed, are, in most European countries, still steeped in ignorance. But what are we to think of men of education—mayors, commissioners of police, lawyers holding high offices—who could believe that the Jews made use of Christian blood in the performance of their religious rites? What are we to think of a public prosecutor who could declare that the Jews wanted Christian blood, and could not have wanted it except for ritual purposes? It is an astonishing instance of how far inveterate prejudice can influence the minds of even educated men.[226]

In Russia, as has been before remarked, the number of the Jews is greater, and the treatment they experience more harsh, than in any other country in the world. From Russia proper—'Holy Russia,' as it is styled— they have been for many generations excluded, nor are they by the law allowed to remain there now. The law is often evaded, and great misery frequently results from it. Some idle or malicious story gains currency, and stirs the populace to a fierce fanatical outbreak, in which pillage, outrage, and massacre are perpetrated on a large scale; or else the authorities are suddenly stirred up to a real or pretended zeal for the vindication of the law, and thousands of Jewish families are all at a moment required to emigrate from the country. In 1846, the Czar Nicholas issued a new ukase, requiring all Jews who dwelt within five-and-thirty miles of the German and Austrian frontier to remove into the interior. The ground alleged for this edict was, that large quantities of goods had been smuggled across the frontier. The English Board of Deputies, among whom were Montefiore and Rothschild, laid a statement before Lord Aberdeen, then Foreign Minister, pointing out the terrible suffering and ruin which this measure would occasion. Lord Aberdeen pleaded their cause with the emperor, who was induced to suspend his ukase, at first for three years, and after that again for four more. Finding that he could not succeed in obtaining its entire revocation, Montefiore made a personal expedition to St. Petersburg, where he was kindly received by the Czar, and succeeded in inducing him to cancel the edict. Under Alexander II. the grievances were in some degree alleviated.

A few have been allowed to leave the old over-crowded settlements, and establish new commercial centres in other provinces of the empire. But their condition is still extremely miserable. They are loaded with special imposts, and subject to all manner of restrictions: they are excluded from many professions, or are only enabled to follow them by paying bribes to officials, who have them completely at their mercy. Fanatical risings against them also are frequent, being connived at, if not actually encouraged, by the authorities.

In Servia, their condition is somewhat better. Forcible emigrations have occasionally occurred, but not to the same extent as in neighbouring countries. Much the same is the case in Moldavia, where they were allowed to follow most handicrafts. It is said that the roofs and pinnacles and churches throughout the country are the work of Jews, and almost every inn has a Jewish landlord. Of late years, however, their privileges have been abridged, and they have been subjected to a good deal of harsh usage.

In Roumania their treatment has been even worse. It may be doubted whether even in Russia the Jews have undergone so many and such undeserved wrongs. It will be remembered that Roumania is the most recently established of all the European kingdoms, having been recognised as an independent State by the Treaty of Berlin in 1878. One of the conditions of their admission to the list of European sovereignties was embodied in Article 44 of the Treaty:—

'In Roumania the difference of religious creeds shall not be alleged against any person as a ground of exclusion from civil and political rights, admission to public employments, and the exercise of professions and industries in any locality whatsoever.'

But the congress had hardly been broken up, when the Roumanians endeavoured to escape from the obligation thus laid upon them. Instead of conferring the privilege of naturalization on the whole of the Jews throughout the country by one sweeping measure, they granted it only to such individuals as applied for it, and required of those certain conditions with which it would be difficult for many Jews, and impossible for many more, to comply.[227] The consequence has been that although there are said to be more than two hundred and fifty thousand Jews in Roumania, who have been for many generations past resident in that country,[228] little more than a thousand have been naturalized; and even in the instance of these, the naturalization is only personal, the children of such persons being reckoned as aliens. In 1884 no single Jew obtained the privilege. In short, the condition on which Roumania was admitted by the Congress of Berlin to rank as a sovereign State has been deliberately and systematically evaded.

This has, indeed, been pointed out to the Roumanian Government by some of the Signatory Powers, but without effect.

It must not be supposed that the withholding of naturalization is merely a sentimental grievance. It entails disabilities of the gravest character, debarring them from most professions and trades, and hampering the Jews seriously in such as they are allowed to follow. No Jew can be a government, a railway, or a sanitary official, a director of a bank, a broker, a clerk, or a chemist. They are excluded from all places of public education; in many places the right of keeping inns has been withdrawn from them; there is a continual agitation in progress to deprive them of the power of carrying on the few trades still allowed them. Only in the year 1884 what was called the 'Hawking Law' was passed, by which hawkers were liable to prosecution if they traded without a licence, and this licence is invariably refused to Jews. Nor does the tale of their wrongs end with their exclusion from all privileges of citizenship. They are exposed to insults and wrongs of all kinds, for which there is practically no redress; no court of law would venture to give an impartial judgment in any suit between a Christian and a Jew.[229] Any attempts to bring the question of their rights before the Senate inevitably fail, permission even to discuss the question being refused. The press, in most countries the advocate of toleration and freedom, is here the bitterest and loudest supporter of injustice and oppression. In fact, the worst intolerance of the worst periods in France, Spain, and Germany is displayed in the Roumania of the present day. It is surprising that the European Powers who imposed their conditions on the Roumanian Government at the Berlin Congress have not felt themselves bound in honour to see them loyally carried out. It may surely be hoped that they will before long awake so far to a sense of their responsibility as to do so.

FOOTNOTES:

[226] See Appendix V., Blood Accusation.

[227] They were required to present petitions, in which the applicant stated the amount of the capital he possessed, and the profession or calling which he followed. After the presentation, he was obliged to reside for *ten years* in the country, during which he must prove himself a useful member of society. It is obvious that in these stipulations there is ample opportunity for refusing naturalization to any Jew whom the Government might dislike.

[228] They are chiefly Sephardim fugitives from Spain in the fifteenth and sixteenth centuries.

[229] At Botouschani, in 1885, five Roumanians were charged with murdering a Jew. The evidence was clear, but the defence was, that a Christian could not be punished for killing a Jew; and a verdict of acquittal was given, but coupled with an order to pay a thousand francs to the Jew's family for the murder. Quite recently an illustrated newspaper issued a large engraving, of which the murder of a Christian child by Jews—the old, shameless, worn-out, a thousand-times-disproved, calumny—was the subject. It is impossible to believe that the proprietors of the paper knew perfectly the falsehood and calumny which they were circulating; but they knew that the bitter hate entertained towards the Jews would ensure them a remunerative sale.

CHAPTER XLIV
A.D. 1800-1885. THE JEWS IN AFRICA, AMERICA, AND ASIA.—CONCLUSION

The position of the Jews in Morocco is less secure than in most Mahometan countries. They suffer from the fanaticism of the Mahometans, who are a less humanized race than their Asiatic brethren. Robbery and murder are perpetrated almost with impunity, the protection of the law being almost a dead letter, so far as they are concerned. As an evidence of their abject condition, it is said that they are compelled to go bare-foot in most of the principal cities. Beyond the bounds of Morocco large numbers of Jews lead a nomad life, dwelling in tents, keeping flocks and herds, and cultivating the land in their vicinity. Their condition in Cairo and Alexandria is somewhat better, and there are many wealthy Jews in these cities. But everywhere they are liable to the outbreaks of blind fanatical fury to which reference has so often been made. An instance of this occurred in 1863, which it is important to notice, as showing only too plainly the condition of things in those countries. A Spaniard had died suddenly at Saffi, and the Spanish authorities required an examination into the circumstances of his death. To avert suspicion from themselves, the Moors accused a Jewish boy, who was in the dead man's service, of poisoning him. He denied the crime, but was scourged until he confessed it, and implicated several other persons. A popular outbreak would have ensued if the Morocco Jews had not appealed to Sir Moses Montefiore. He requested the intervention of our Government, and made an expedition to Morocco, where he not only succeeded in releasing several Jews, who had been detained in prison on charges which could not be proved, but obtained an audience of the Sultan of Morocco, who received him with great distinction. He pointed out to the Sultan that the Jews of Morocco were without any legal protection, and were in consequence frequently subject to outrages for which they could obtain no redress; and he entreated that equal justice might be secured to them as to other inhabitants of the country. In a few days an edict was issued, commanding that in future Jews, Christians, and Mahometans should be treated with equal justice throughout the Sultan's dominions. Experience has shown that it is more easy to obtain these concessions from Moslem sovereigns than to ensure their due observance by subordinate officers. Still, there can be no doubt that this is a great advance in the social condition of the Jews of Morocco.

There are a good many Jews in Brazil and in the United States of America. In the last-named country it needs not to be said that they enjoy the most entire toleration. Jewish hospitals, Jewish orphanages, free schools, almshouses, benevolent institutions of all kinds, exist in the principal cities, in which also magnificent synagogues are to be found. The authority of the Rabbins, however, is not so great, as a rule, as it is in European countries. It is said that there is great laxity in their ritual—some discarding Hebrew altogether in their liturgies, some making the Sunday instead of the Saturday their day of religious observance. Their increase of population during the last few generations has been extraordinarily rapid. Jews are found scattered in Mexico and in the great South American cities, but not in any great numbers.

In the dominions of the Sultan, both the European and the Asiatic, the position of the Jews during the present century has varied little from what it was in those which preceded it. As has been already remarked, they are more kindly and fairly treated than in other Mahometan countries— the result, probably, of freer communication with Europe. But here, too, they are liable to sudden outbursts of religious fanaticism or commercial jealousy, and on these occasions they suffer great injustice and cruelty. Two signal instances of this occurred a.d. 1840.

In that year, a Greek boy in the island of Rhodes having suddenly disappeared, a woman affirmed that she had seen him, shortly before, in company with a Jew. It chanced to be near the time of the Passover, and, strange as it may seem, some of the European consuls, on no better evidence than this, raised the old slander that the boy had been murdered, in order that his blood might be used for ritual purposes. The Jew was arrested, and denied any knowledge of the boy. He was thereupon put to the torture, under which his reason gave way, and he uttered the names of several Jews, who were at once assumed to be his accomplices. They were seized, and in their turn put on the rack; the Jewish quarter was closed, and no food allowed to enter it; and it is even said that an attempt was made to convey a dead body into one of the houses, in order that it might be found there. The story spread in all directions, and popular risings and outrages on the Jews ensued.

The affair at Damascus was even more serious. Father Tomaso, a monk, who for many years had practised medicine, suddenly disappeared. A report was spread that he had been last seen in the Jewish quarter, which was instantly invaded by a mob of Christians, who denounced the Jews as his murderers. Count Menton, the French Consul, actuated, it is believed, by political motives, took up the matter and insisted on the punishment of the offenders, as he chose to consider the Jews. He produced persons who swore that the monk had been seen to enter the shop of a Jewish barber, from which he had never issued forth again. The barber was seized and bastinadoed, until in his agony he accused several of the richest Jews in the city as having been concerned in the murder. They were subjected in their turn to tortures, under which two of them died, and several more confessed their complicity in the crime. A young Jew, who swore that he had seen Father Tomaso enter the house of a Turkish merchant, on the evening of his disappearance, was bastinadoed to death, in order to induce him to retract his statement. The French Consul now laid the confessions which had been extracted from the prisoners before the Turkish Pacha, and insisted on their being immediately put to death.

Fortunately the Pacha thought it his safer course to apply to head quarters for instructions, and thus sufficient time was given for the report of what had occurred to reach England. There it created a profound sensation. A large meeting of influential Jews was held in London, at the house of Sir Moses Montefiore, who was deputed to seek an interview with Lord Palmerston, at that time Foreign Secretary. From him Sir Moses received all possible help; but it was thought advisable that a special mission should be sent to the East to represent the matter in its true light to the Turkish authorities. Sir Moses himself undertook the office, and proceeded to Syria, accompanied by M. Cremieux, a Jewish member of the French Chamber, and several others. They learned that at Rhodes the prisoners had been liberated, and the governor who had sanctioned the proceedings dismissed from his office; but the Damascus affair was still undetermined. Sir Moses obtained an interview with the Pacha of Egypt, who endeavoured to compromise the matter by offering to pardon all the prisoners who had been accused. But he was answered that it was not justice to pardon innocent men. What was demanded was a complete and honourable acquittal of the accused. This was presently granted, and the prisoners discharged from custody. Subsequently Sir Moses had an interview with the Sultan himself, on the 6th of November in the same year, 1840, when he obtained from him—as he had formerly done from the Sultan of Morocco—the celebrated firman, which granted to the Jews, everywhere throughout the Turkish dominions, the most complete protection.

In Persia, Bokhara, Yemen, and Central Asia, numerous colonies of Jews exist, engaged as a rule in trade, but also occasionally employed in agriculture. They are not as wealthy, apparently, as their Western brethren.

Many of them, indeed, are extremely poor, earning their subsistence as day labourers. They speak and write their own language only, though able to converse with the inhabitants of the country. They live very much among themselves, never intermarrying with strangers, and carry their differences to the Rabbi of their synagogue, who, indeed, is the judge authorized by the law for the settlement of their disputes. One cause of their isolation is their fear of allowing their children to study secular subjects, which they think would be likely to undermine the foundations of their faith.

In the Holy Land, it was reported in 1881 that there were about 15,000 Jews in Jerusalem, about half its population. Whether that is correct or not, it is certain that the number of Jews in that city is steadily, though not rapidly, increasing, and has been on the increase ever since the Crimean War. Whatever may be thought about that war, one of its consequences was to open Palestine to European settlers; and, as might have been expected, the Jews availed themselves of the opportunity of obtaining for themselves a home in the ancient land of their fathers. But very few of those who have attempted this possessed the means of comfortably establishing themselves. It has been remarked by one who knows the Jews well, that they are contented to live elsewhere so long as life goes prosperously with them. It is the poor, the unfortunate, the persecuted, who seek a refuge there. Old people again, whose children are out in the world, come to spend the remainder of their days in religious exercises. A few Rabbins also devote themselves to the work of looking after the various communities thus established. The Montefiore Testimonial Committee has done something to assist this immigration. It has established agricultural communities in various places, notably beyond the western walls of Jerusalem, where four thousand Jews are lodged in comfortable houses, especially built for them. The population has trebled itself, according to trustworthy information, since 1860.

But there are great drawbacks. The Jews are not naturally disposed to manual labour, preferring, as they themselves say, to work with their brains rather than their hands. There is also the temptation—which always besets those who live, to some extent, on the charity of others—to abuse the generosity of their benefactors, by doing no work at all themselves. There is also the competition of the native labourer, the fellah, who is used to the climate, and hard labour and poor food, and who can live at about one-third of what is necessary for the Jew. On the whole, it cannot be said that the lower classes of Jews are prospering in the Holy Land.

There are, however, many synagogues both of Ashkenazim and Sephardim Jews in Jerusalem, and Talmudical schools supported by large contributions levied on Jews throughout the world. Schools also exist at Hebron, Tiberias, Safed, Jaffa, and other towns. There are also three Jewish hospitals in Jerusalem, as well as numerous almshouses. All sects of Jews are represented in Jerusalem, Chasidim and Karaites, as well as the orthodox adherents of the Rabbins. On the whole, though there is no doubt that the condition of the Palestinian Jews has been ameliorated of late years, it is still doubtful whether any permanent improvement can be effected while the country continues to be subject to Turkish misrule.

Here, then, we bring to an end this strangely varied, yet still more strangely monotonous, narrative—not, as in the case of any other ancient people, because its national history has come to an end, but simply because we cannot read the future. Eighteen centuries have, in all other instances, effected so vast a change in the condition of a nation, that it is difficult to trace any identity between its earlier and its later generations. Eighteen centuries ago our own ancestors were savage tribes, living in wattled huts, staining their naked bodies with woad, and practising barbarous and bloody rites. In language, in religion, in mental and moral culture, in social organization, they were so wholly different from ourselves that it is difficult to discover any point of resemblance between the two. But in all these respects, the Jew of the first century differs but little from his descendant eighteen hundred years afterwards. He speaks the same tongue, he holds the same creed, he observes the same habits, or nearly the same habits, of life as his forefathers did all that long period ago. And yet that long period is not half the life of the Jewish people. It began in an age when the tradition of the Flood was still fresh on earth; it is still in the fulness of its life, when the eye of faith can distinguish, not very far off, the dawning of the Judgment Day. How is this strange tale to end? What is to be the last act of this amazing drama? Jerusalem has been long trodden down of the Gentiles; the times of the Gentiles are nearly fulfilled. What is to follow? Are the Jews to be restored, as a distinct people, to the Land of Promise, and there accept Him whom their fathers rejected as their King? There is no subject on which speculation is more busy, or on which more confident judgments are pronounced. But it is the voice of man that speaks, not of God. One thing alone is sure. God has not cast away His people. Who can read their history, and doubt that? But when, where, or how, He may be pleased to take them again into favour, no man can foretell. Our children will behold the solution of the riddle, and bless God for His mercy. Let us, too, bless God, and wait in faith.

APPENDIX I
STATISTICS OF JEWISH POPULATION

It is always difficult to determine the number of Jews resident either in the Holy Land or in any other country of the world. The remark applies to ancient, even more than modern, times. It is not only that the information afforded by writers is scanty, but that the statements made by some historians differ greatly from those supplied by others; while a good deal must be rejected as wholly incredible. To take an instance, we are informed by the author of the Book of Samuel,[230] that the military population of David's kingdom was 1,300,000. But in the parallel passage in the Book of Chronicles[231] the number is stated to be nearly 300,000 more. 'To attempt reconciling these discrepancies,' says an intelligent writer,[232] 'would be wasted labour.' During the reign of Rehoboam, b.c. 975, the number of the men of Judah who drew the sword is rated at 180,000.[233] But at the accession of his son, not twenty years afterwards, it is 400,000.[234] Whether we are to attribute these contradictions to corruptions of the text or to different modes of calculation, signifies little to us. The two statements are quite irreconcilable with one another. Josephus's numbers, again, are wholly untrustworthy. He reckons the sum of those who returned with Zorobabel from Babylon, at the enormous figure of 4,628,000 and 47,000 women.[235] This is, of course, an absolute impossibility; and we know, from the books of Ezra and Nehemiah, that the real amount was 42,000. [236] It has been suggested that Josephus's text is corrupt in this passage. But if so, it may well be assumed to be corrupt in other similar places also. Thus he affirms that the numbers shut up in Jerusalem during the siege by Titus was 2,700,000,[237] while the estimate of Tacitus is 600,000.[238] Here again, though the reckoning of the Roman historian is probably below the mark, he having omitted to allow for the unusual number of residents at the time of the siege, yet that of Josephus must be rejected as incredible. [239] The circumference of the walls of Jerusalem is generally admitted to have been about four miles. The space thus enclosed within the walls would be about equal to that part of the area of London which extends from Tyburn Gate to the British Museum in one direction, and from the Regent's Park to Whitehall in the other, drawing an imaginary circle, of which the Regent's Circus would be the centre. The portion thus enclosed—hardly one tenth part of what lies within the bills of mortality—may contain half a million persons. Allowing for the narrow streets of old Jerusalem, we may reckon that the same area in that city would hold 100,000 more, thus very nearly verifying the statement of Tacitus. No doubt, at the time of the Passover, vast numbers came from foreign lands, and these found accommodation, as well as they could, in Jerusalem itself, or in the environs. Many probably were lodged in outlying villages, and many more, according to the common practice in the East, slept in the open air. These would, of course, be driven into Jerusalem by the approach of the Roman armies, and thus the numbers at the beginning of the siege might have amounted to a million or thereabouts. But the notion of nearly three millions being crowded into the area above described is simply preposterous.

But if Josephus's statistics on these two important points are to be rejected as wholly untrustworthy, how are we to credit his assertions in matters of very nearly the same kind? He tells us that Galilee in his time contained more than two hundred towns and villages, no one of which held less than 15,000 inhabitants.[240] If this were indeed the case, that province, scarcely larger than one of the largest of our English counties, must have had a population of fully three millions, while that of the whole of Palestine would approach ten millions. Few readers will be found to credit this.

At the same time more than one trustworthy writer affirms that Palestine was a thickly populated country. The population to the square mile is said to have been larger in it than in any other portion of the Roman dominions. Diodorus,[241] Strabo,[242] Tacitus,[243] and Dion Cassius[244] all concur in this; and therefore, though we cannot accept Josephus's statements as being even approximately accurate, they may be admitted so far, as establishing the numerous population of Palestine at the time of the siege. Nor are we wholly without means of forming an estimate as to its amount, independently altogether of the above-named writers. Thus Hecatæus of Abdera (quoted by Joseph. Ap. i. 21) says that Jerusalem in his time (a.d. 312) contained 120,000 inhabitants. Presuming the average increase of population to have taken place, according to this reckoning, Jerusalem at the time of the siege would contain about 600,000—agreeing closely with Tacitus's estimate. According to Maccab. II., the city at the date of Antiochus Epiphanes, a.d. 180, had 160,000, or, according to others, 180,000. This would make the number of residents at the outbreak of the civil war somewhat less; but there would be no material difference. On the whole, we may assume that, by dividing Josephus's estimates by three, we approximate to the real number. According to this, the census of the Holy Land, a.d. 71, would be about three and a half millions, and the total of persons besieged in the Holy City something under one million.

It is still more difficult to estimate the total of the Jews in other countries of the world at this time. We may safely assume that they could not have been fewer than the inhabitants of Palestine. We have reason to believe that the bulk of the nation did not return with Zorobabel. Those who remained behind in the foreign countries to which they had been conveyed throve and multiplied in their new homes. There are grounds for supposing that, at subsequent periods, large emigrations from the Holy Land took place, probably at the date of King Ahasuerus's edict, more certainly during the persecution of Antiochus Epiphanes and the Roman invasion. We have the clearest testimony of contemporaneous writers as to the extent to which the Jews in our Lord's time had spread into foreign lands, forming everywhere a distinct people, as they do at the present day. Mommsen quotes the statement of a writer of Julius Cæsar's date, to the effect that it would be dangerous for the Roman governor of his province to offend the Jews, because, on his return to Rome, he might encounter contumely from their countrymen there. Agrippa I. wrote to the Emperor Caligula to the same effect, but more explicitly. 'Jerusalem,' he says, 'is the metropolis, not of Judæa only, but of very many lands, on account of the colonies which from time to time it has sent out into the adjoining countries—Egypt, Phœnicia, Syria, Cœlo-Syria, Pamphylia, Cilicia, Asia Minor, as far as Bithynia, and the remotest parts of Pontus; likewise into Europe—Thessaly, Bœotia, Macedonia, Ætolia, Attica, Argos, Corinth, and the Peloponnesus. Nor are the Jewish settlements confined to the mainland. They are to be found also in the more important islands, Eubœa, Cyprus, Crete. I do not insist on the countries beyond the Euphrates; for with few exceptions all of them, Babylon and the fertile regions round it, have Jewish inhabitants.'[245] This testimony is confirmed by St. Luke's narrative of what occurred on the day of Pentecost immediately following the crucifixion (Acts ii. 9, 10). It can hardly be doubted that at the date of the commencement of this history, there were fully as many Jews in other lands as there were in Palestine—the whole nation numbering, at the lowest computation, not less than seven millions.

Eighteen centuries have elapsed since that time, and the Jews are still a distinct and peculiar people, intermarrying with other races less than any other nation in the world. According to the rate[246] at which population ordinarily increases, they ought to have doubled their number more than seven times over, and to amount at the present time to many hundreds of millions. The inherent vigour of the race does not seem to be either intellectually or physically impaired. It is reported by those who have studied the question, that their health, in the various lands where they are sojourners, is at least as good, indeed, distinctly better, than that of the populations among which they reside. It becomes, then, an interesting and curious question—what the amount of their numbers is in the present day. Nor does the same difficulty we have experienced in endeavouring to ascertain the exact sum of their population at the time of the fall of Jerusalem, meet us when we enter on that. Statistics have been given by trustworthy authorities, which are found, on examination, to agree very nearly with one another. I propose to give them here in detail.

To begin with Europe. Here the country in which they are most numerous is Russia. In that, the official return for 1876 was 2,612,179. In Austria and Hungary it was 1,372,333; in the German Empire, 520,575. In France their total does not exceed 60,000 or 80,000.[247] In England, the number is nearly the same. In Italy the total is 53,000; in Holland, 68,000; in Moldavia, Servia, and Roumania, about 300,000. In the remaining countries of Europe there may be 20,000. These returns show a total of some hundreds of thousands over 5,000,000 of Jews in Europe.

Proceeding to Asia, the Jews in the Turkish dominions (including both Turkey in Europe and Turkey in Asia) amount to about 200,000. In Persia, Bokhara, Samarcand, Central and Eastern Asia, it is more difficult to ascertain their real numbers; but it is generally agreed that these may be approximately estimated at 50,000. In Arabia, there is a great difference of opinion, some affirming them to amount to as many as 200,000, while more trustworthy authorities place the total at one tenth that number. There are also the Jews of Syria and the Holy Land, of which the census has already been given. On the whole, the Asiatic Jews may be considered as amounting to 300,000, or perhaps 400,000.

Turning next to Africa, the Jews of Egypt are estimated at 80,000; those of Tripoli, 100,000; of Tunis, 50,000; of Algiers, 70,000; of Morocco, 300,000. Thus the total of African Jews in the Northern kingdoms somewhat exceeds half a million. If to these are added such as are to be found in Central and Southern Africa, the entire sum may amount to 600,000.

Lastly, in America and Australia there is said to be a Jewish population somewhat exceeding that of Asia. Here their chief centres are the United States, Canada, and Brazil.

From these returns, which, it may be assumed, are neither much in excess nor much short of the actual amount, the total number of professing Jews at the present time appears to be somewhat less than seven millions—the very number which, so far as it is possible to determine, was that of the Jewish people when the Lord became incarnate upon earth. Can any man realize this astonishing fact, and yet doubt the living miracle which the history of the Jews presents?

> 'How many generations of mankind
> Have risen and fallen asleep,
> Yet it remains the same!'

FOOTNOTES:

[230] 2 Sam. xxiv. 9.

[231] 1 Chron. xxi. 5.

[232] Adam Clarke.

[233] 1 Kings xii. 21.

[234] 2 Chron. xiii. 3.

[235] Joseph., *Ant.* xi. 3, § 10.

[236] Ezra ii. 64; Nehem. vii. 66.

[237] Joseph., *Bell. Jud.* vi. 9, § 3.

[238] Tac. *Hist.* v. 13.

[239] This is the most probable explanation of the smallness of his estimate of the numbers in the city during the siege. The ordinary population would probably be about the amount he gives.

[240] Joseph., *Bell. Jud.* iii. 3, § 2.

[241] Diodor. Sic. xl. *Eclog.* 1.

[242] Strabo xvi. 2, § 28.

[243] Tacitus, *Hist.* v. 8.

[244] Dion Cass. lxix. 14. Dion makes the astonishing assertion that Adrian destroyed nearly 1000 towns κῶμαι ὀνομαστοτόται in Palestine, besides fortresses.

[245] Philo, *Legat. ad Gaium*, § 36.

[246] The increase of population is said by those who have made the subject their study, to be 1/227 annually, or according to others, 1/223.

[247] This is probably too low an estimate. In a census taken in 1808, there were 80,000 Jews in France; and there has been nothing to check their increase. Their number is more probably 100,000.

APPENDIX II
THE TALMUDS

The word Talmud has several meanings, which are most nearly rendered by 'study,' or 'learning.' There are two books so called—the Jerusalem and the Babylonian. Each of these is made up of two parts—the Mishna, or repetition,—it being, as it were, a reissue of the Mosaic law,—and the Gemara, or complement, the critical expansion of the Mishna. The Mishna of both Talmuds is the same, the Gemaras different: that of the Babylonian being the larger as well as the more diversified. They are encyclopædias of the Jewish knowledge of their day, and deal with civil and criminal, as well as moral and religious questions, law, science, metaphysics, history, and general literature.

The Mishna was compiled by Rabbi Judah, called Hakkadosh, or 'the Holy,' who lived in the reign of Antoninus Pius. It is written in very pure Hebrew. But as many things are introduced into it which have foreign names, there is a frequent occurrence of Latin and Greek phrases. The Gemara of the Jerusalem Talmud, which is believed to have been completed about the end of the fourth century, is written in what is called the Eastern Aramæan: that of the Babylonian, which is at the least a century, and probably two centuries, later, in Western Aramæan.

The origin of the Mishna is declared to be as follows. While Moses was with God in Sinai, He communicated to him a twofold law, written and oral. [248] The latter Moses repeated to Aaron, who delivered it to Eleazar and Ithamar; they to the Seventy Elders; they to the prophets; and the prophets to the synagogues. In this manner it was passed on from generation to generation, to the time of the great Jewish doctor Hillel, who lived shortly before the birth of Christ. He digested the great mass of precepts under six heads, still, however, without committing them to writing; which, it was believed, would have been contrary to the intention of the Divine Giver. Under the more formal shape which it had now assumed, the Oral Law was passed on till the time of the destruction of Bethor, and the final dispersion of the Hebrew people. Then, as we have seen, Rabbi Judah Hakkadosh, perceiving that the restoration of the Jews to their ancient status was not to be looked for, and fearing that the consequence of this would be the total loss of the 'Law of the Mouth,' as it was called,—conceiving also that the peculiar circumstances of the case justified him in breaking the rule that had been so long observed,—embodied the traditions in a volume which might be preserved for ever, secure from addition or change.

His countrymen endorsed this belief, and accepted the Mishna with the most profound respect. It had scarcely been issued, when commentaries began to be written upon it by learned Rabbins; which, about the end of the third century, were collected into a volume by Rabbi Jochanan Ben Eliezer, and called the Gemara. The style in which this is written is harsh, much inferior to that of the Mishna; and even the best Hebraists are unable to expound satisfactorily some portions of it. This obscurity was probably the reason why another Gemara was set on foot by the Mesopotamian Jews, about a century after the issue of the Jerusalem Talmud. The work was begun by Rabbi Asa or Asche, and carried on to the time of Rabbi Jose, about a.d. 500. There is some variety of opinion as to the date of its completion; but Laurence is generally thought to have proved satisfactorily that it cannot be later than the beginning of the sixth century. Christian commentators commonly prefer the Jerusalem Talmud,[249] as containing less of fabulous and frivolous matter; but the preference of the Jews is for that of Babylon.

The Mishna is divided into six principal heads, or Orders, as they are called. Each Order is divided into a variety of titles or treatises, and these again into chapters and sections. The six Orders are: I. Zeraim, or Seeds; II. Moed, or Festivals; III. Nashim, or Women; IV. Nezikin, or Injuries; V. Kodashim, or Holy Things; and VI. Taharoth, or Purifications.

The First Order is subdivided into eleven treatises:—

1. Treats of the prayers and benedictions which are to precede and follow meals.

2. Of the gleanings of vine and olive yards, alms, and first-fruits to be given to the poor.

3. Of the purchased fruits of the earth, which may be lawfully used, if they have paid tithe, but are illegal if they have not paid.

4. Of mixtures of various kinds of grain, and the wool of animals.

5. Of the laws relating to the Sabbatic, or seventh, year.

6. Of the first-fruits, given to the Priests.

7. Of the tithes, given to the Levites.

8. Of the second tithe, to be sent up to Jerusalem.

9. Of the cake offered as a heave offering.

10. Of the fruits of trees to be counted as uncircumcised for three years.

11. Of first-fruits generally.

The Second Order contains thirteen treatises:—

1. Of the Sabbath day.

2. Of various Sabbatical rules.

3. Of the Passover.

4. Of the half shekel paid as tribute to the Sanctuary.

5. Of the great Day of Atonement.

6. Of the Feast of Tabernacles.

7. Of Pentecost.

8. Of certain things forbidden on Feast Days.

9. Of the New Year.

10. Of the Fasts and Days of Humiliation.

11. Of the Feast of Purim. 12. Of the lesser Jewish Festivals.

13. Of the three great Festivals.

The Third Order has seven titles:—

1. Of the Law of Levitical Marriage.

2. Of Marriage Contracts.

3. Of Women's Vows.

4. Of the Vows of Nazarites.

5. Of Writings of Divorcement.

6. Of the Putting away of Wives.

7. Of the Ceremony of Espousal.

The Fourth Order has nine sections:—

1. Injuries inflicted by Violence, Wounds, etc.

2. Leases, Hirings, Loans, Exchanges, etc.

3. Succession to Property, Partnerships, Contracts, etc.

4. The Sanhedrin.

5. Stripes.

6. Oaths.

7. Witnesses, Evidence, also Idolatry.[250]

8. Decrees of Judges and Apothegms of Wise Men.

9. Record of Errors in the Decisions of Judges.

The Fifth runs to eleven treatises, which deal with:—

1. Sacrifices.

2. Oblations and Offerings.

3. Things Profane.

4. The First Born.

5. Valuations of Males and Females.

6. Exchange and Redemption.

7. Atoning Sacrifices.

8. Trespass Offerings.

9. The Daily Sacrifice.

10. Dimensions, Form, and Structure of the Sanctuary.

11. Offerings of Birds.

The Sixth and last Order contains twelve heads, relating to:—

1. Purifying of Vessels.

2. Tents and Tabernacles, and Pollution by Corpses.

3. Vestments and Uncleanness by Leprosy.

4. The Ashes of the Heifer Purifying the Unclean.

5. Purifications generally.

6. Vessels containing Water.

7. Separation for Legal Impurity.

8. Legal Impurity generally.

9. Regulations concerning Uncleanness.

10. The Washing of Lepers.

11. The Washing of Hands.

12. Supplementary matters.

The Gemaras, it should be noted, are not so much commentaries on the Mishna, as a series of disquisitions on passages in Holy Scripture, or on the text of the Mishna, or possibly on some question of Jewish law. Great subtlety of thought is displayed in these discussions. Points of similarity are discovered between things which are, to ordinary observation, wholly diverse, and points of difference between things apparently quite identical. The ruling principle of the writers seems to be, that in the sacred writings, and more particularly in the Pentateuch, there is not a word, not a letter, that has not its special use and significance. Where this is not patent or easy of discovery, they hold that it is nevertheless latent in the text, and will be brought out when events have taken place, or opinions have been propounded, which were necessary to its development—as what appears to be a mere speck in a photograph may be enlarged until it is found to be in itself a complete picture. These lengthy and abstruse speculations are frequently varied by incidental anecdotes (called Haggadoth), which serve to illustrate the writer's meaning, by allegories, proverbs and parables, or sometimes by the wildest Oriental legends, myths, and romantic tales. Some of these are extremely touching and beautiful; others absurd, frivolous, and extravagant, bordering occasionally on the profane, if not the blasphemous. There is, in fact, a strange and bizarre mixture of heterogeneous subjects. Eastern fancies are intermingled with the speculations of the Greek and Roman moralists. A celebrated writer has described the Talmud as 'an extraordinary monument of human industry, human wisdom, and human folly.'[251] The probable explanation of this perversion of high intellect and patient study is to be found in the fact that the writers, being excluded by the peculiarity of their social and political position from handling the topics on which literary men ordinarily employ their pens, they were driven to busy themselves with the only subjects open to them. Hence too, probably, the extraordinary respect paid to the Talmuds by the Jewish people. They have ever regarded these books, and especially the Babylonian Talmud, with the profoundest reverence and affection. Indeed, they have been charged with bestowing more of their regard on them than on their own inspired Scriptures. They have a proverb, that 'They who study the Scriptures do a virtuous, but not an unmixedly virtuous, act. They who study the Mishna perform a wholly virtuous act, and merit a reward. But they who study the Gemara perform the most virtuous of all acts.' And again, 'The Scriptures are water, the Mishna wine, the Gemara spiced wine.'[252]

As regards the history of the Talmuds, it is a singular fact that no notice is taken of either Mishna or Gemara by any of the Fathers belonging to the first four centuries of Church history, notwithstanding that they frequently handle the subject of Jewish tradition. Even Tertullian, when specially writing on this subject, while he speaks of the primal law given to Adam, and the laws of the Two Tables committed to Moses, makes no mention of the Mishna. Augustine, in the fifth century, does name the δευτέρωσις, or Second Law; but even he speaks of it as containing the *unwritten* traditions of the Jews, transmitted from one generation to another by word of mouth. We can only suppose that, although the Mishna was indeed completed before the end of the second century, the knowledge of it was for a long time confined to the learned among the Jews, and for a still longer time to the Hebrew nation generally. The same was the case as regards the completed Jerusalem Talmud. There was, in fact, no recognition of the work by Christians until the time of the Emperor Justinian, who, about the middle of the sixth century, issued a Novella, or edict, against it. He allowed the reading of Scripture in the synagogues, but prohibited that of the Mishna, as being 'the mere invention of earthly men, who had nothing of Heaven in them.' From his time to the sixteenth century of Christianity, popes and kings have put forth one manifesto after another, warning men against its perusal, and ordering the book itself to be suppressed, and even publicly destroyed. In 1286 Pope Honorius IV. wrote to Archbishop Peckham, requiring him to forbid the perusal of the Talmud as a 'liber damnabilis,' from which all of manner of evil was certain to arise. Nor were the popes content with prescribing it. In 1230 Gregory IX., following the example of his predecessor Innocent, burned twenty cartloads of it. In 1553, during the Feast of Tabernacles, all the copies that could anywhere be found were committed to the flames by order of Julius III.; and a few years subsequently, 12,000 volumes underwent the same fate by command of Paul IV. During the last half of the sixteenth century the Talmud was in this manner brought to the stake no less than six times, and was burned, not by the single copy, but by the waggonload. The Hebrew copyists of those times must have laboured hard to prevent the total disappearance of the book. But the establishment of the printing presses, and the declaration of Reuchlin, early in the sixteenth century, in its favour, in the course of a generation or two put an end to the attempts to root out all traces of it.

The celebrated Maimonides, in the twelfth century, made an epitome of the laws of the Talmud, which many prefer to the Talmud itself, forasmuch as he omits the strange fables with which the original work abounds, and preserves the really valuable matter. The name of his book is Yad-ha-chazzak, or *The Strong Hand*. It is of great use to those who wish to gain a knowledge of Jewish laws and ceremonies.

FOOTNOTES:

[248] The meaning of this is, that the development of the Law is contained in the Law itself. There must have been from the first difficulties in the interpretation of the Law. These were referred to Moses. His decisions were traditionally preserved, and called the Oral Law, this is figured by God's delivering the Oral Law to Moses. A Rabbinical fable further declares that God committed the Written Law to Moses by day, and the Oral by night. This symbolizes, first, that God's law is the true measure of time, and secondly, that the Written Law is to the Oral as the light to the darkness.

[249] The Jerusalem Talmud contains only four of the six Orders which make up that of Babylon, and a portion of the fifth. Whenever, it should be noted, 'The Talmud' is spoken of, without any intimation *which* Talmud is referred to, the expression must be understood to mean that of Babylon.

[250] Here introduced because idolatry is sometimes the subject of judicial proceedings.

[251] Against this, however, may be set the opinion of the celebrated Buxtorf. He says, that 'it contains excellent lessons in jurisprudence, medicine, physics, ethics, politics, and astronomy; admirable proverbs, and apothegms and shining gems of eloquence, not less ornamental to the

Hebrew tongue than are the flowers of eloquence to the Greek and Latin languages. Nor would the knowledge of Hebrew and Chaldee be complete without them.'

[252] Some persons might be inclined to remark on this saying, that it is a great deal truer than its authors were aware of. Yet its meaning has probably been misunderstood, and there is no intention of disparaging Scripture. It may only mean, that the Mishna is the knowledge of Scripture with more knowledge added, and the Gemara is the knowledge of Scripture and Mishna combined with a yet further addition of knowledge.

APPENDIX III
THE TARGUMS, MASSORA, CABBALA, SEPHER-YETZIRA, AND ZOHAR

THE TARGUMS

The Targums are expository paraphrases of the Books of the Old Testament. They are written in Chaldee, which was more familiar to the Jews after Ezra's time than the Hebrew. It would appear that after the return from Captivity it was the habit in the synagogue worship to read out some portion of Scripture in the Hebrew, and then give orally a Targum on the passage in question. But the *written* Targums—viz., those of Jonathan, Onkelos, Jonathan son of Uzziel, Jerusalem, and Joseph the Blind—were none of them composed, or at all events committed to writing, much before the era of our Lord. They come therefore within the scope of the present work.

The Targum of Jonathan is the most ancient, and is generally thought to have been drawn up in its present form about thirty years before the birth of Christ. That of Onkelos is somewhat later, and is concerned with the Books of Moses only. It is greatly superior to its predecessor in simplicity of language and purity of style. It is quoted in the Mishna, but does not seem to have been known to the early Christian Fathers.

The Targum of the younger Jonathan comments on the Books of the Prophets only. It resembles that of Onkelos in purity of style, but is less simple, and runs occasionally into allegory. It is believed that additions have been made to it by doctors who lived long subsequently to its author.

The Targum of Jerusalem deals with the Books of Moses, or rather with a portion of them. It is little better than a fragment of an ancient paraphrase of the Pentateuch.

The Targum of Joseph the Blind is on the Hagiographa, viz., the Psalms, Proverbs, Ecclesiastes, Song of Solomon, Esther, Job, and Ruth. The style is very corrupt Chaldee, containing many foreign words.

There is no Targum on Daniel, Ezra, or Nehemiah, because these books were already written in Aramaic. The Targums are of much value in establishing the genuineness of the present Hebrew text, proving it to be the same as it was when the Targums were written. They are also useful in Jewish controversy, as showing the manner in which the Jews, previously to the Christian era, interpreted the great prophecies respecting the Messiah.

MASSORA

This word properly denotes tradition; and those persons are called Massorites who determined the meaning of the Hebrew text by adding pointed vowels to it. There are in the Hebrew language four vowels, but these were found insufficient; and further, it was a frequent practice in early times to omit these vowels, writing the consonants only of the words. The consequence of this was, that the meaning of a word was often ambiguous, its sense becoming different according to the vowels inserted. Thus there is said to have been a dispute between David and Joab as to the meaning of the word רנז (Deut. xxv. 19). In one of his raids against the Amalekites, Joab slew the men, but spared the women and children. David rebuked him for this, alleging that the command was 'to blot out the memory of,' i.e., to exterminate (הֲזֵן) the Amalekites. But Joab answered that the word was הֲזָ, ordering the slaughter of the males only.[254] In order to put a stop to perplexities so caused, the Massorites[255] are said to have added the points, or pointed vowels, of which there are fourteen. These are placed below or above the consonants, supplying the place of vowels, where these are wanting, and determining the pronunciation, when present.

The Massorites not only added the vowel points, but numbered the chapters, sections, verses, words, and even the letters of the sacred text. Thus they have noted the fact that there are in the Book of Genesis 1,534 verses, 20,713 words, and 78,100 letters. They have also marked the central verse, word, and letter of the book. They have done the same also in the instance of all the other Books of the Old Testament. The object is to preserve the inspired text from interpolation, mutilation, in fact, change of any kind, and also to give facilities for reference. Much of their work has been censured as 'laborious trifling;' but it has been of service to scholars nevertheless.

The age to be assigned to the Massorites is a matter of doubt. Some have affirmed that Moses himself communicated to the elders this method of elucidating and preserving inviolate the Sacred Writings. Others ascribe the invention of the Massoretic vowels to Ezra, and the Great Synagogue of his time. But neither of these opinions has much to support it; and the most trustworthy authorities place them in the fifth or sixth century of Christianity. The fact that there were many variations in the sacred text long subsequently to the time of Ezra, is clearly enough proved by the versions of the Septuagint writers, Aquila, Symmachus and Theodotion, none of which are in entire accordance with one another. This could not have been the case if, previously to the date of these translators, the Massorites had completed their labours. Jerome states that the text was not determined even in his time. The most approved view seems to be that of Walton. He thinks that the work was begun early in the fifth century, and came gradually more into notice, until it was completed, *circa* 1030 a.d. Maimonides appears to say that the final revision was made by the famous scholar Rabbi Ben Asher. The Massorites, it should be noted, have been charged with endeavouring to pass off erroneous readings favourable to their own views, and, in order to secure this object, preventing any recurrence to the original and genuine text.

CABBALA

This word also denotes tradition, and originally included all the interpretations of Scripture, which the Jews professed to have received, in the first instance, from Moses, and in the second, from Ezra. But subsequently it came to be used for an abstruse species of science, by which certain passages of Holy Writ are mystically explained. The Cabbala, in this sense, has many processes, of which the three best known are Gematria, Notaricon, and Themurah.[256] The first mentioned of these consists in assuming the letters of a Hebrew word to denote ciphers, or arithmetical numbers, and then explaining every word by the arithmetical value of the letters composing it. Thus, for example, the letters of the word Jabo-Shiloh (Gen. xlix. 10), that is, 'Shiloh shall come,' when reckoned according to their arithmetical valuation, make up the same number as does the Hebrew word 'Messiah.' Hence the Cabbalists infer that Shiloh signifies the same as Messiah.

Notaricon consists in taking every letter of a word as being in itself a complete word, and the letters, when put together, as a complete sentence. Thus, the first word of the Book of Genesis, Bereshith, resolved into its component letters, is understood to mean Bara, Rakia, Arez, Shamaion, Iam, Tehomoth, *i.e.,* 'He created the firmament, the earth, the heavens, the sea, and the deep.' Or again, the initial letters of every word in a sentence may be formed into a word, possessing, of course, a mystical meaning.

Themurah, is where the letters are transposed so as to form a new word—sometimes by the process known to us as anagram, sometimes by the substitution of one letter for another. The Cabbalists believed that the Scriptures contained endless recondite meanings, which might be brought to light by patient investigation. They were persuaded that the sacred writers had some special secret reason for their choice of every word they employed, and for its place in the verse, chapter, and book in which it is found.

BOOK OF YETZIRA

Though some of the Chasidim professed a reverence for the Talmud, their system of theology is in reality antagonistic to it.[257] The basis of their confession of faith is, not the Talmud, but the Book of Zohar. This, together with the Yetzira, contains the fullest exposition of their views.

The age of the Sepher-Yetzira, Book of Creation, is a matter of dispute. By many it has been assigned to the seventh or eighth century. More trustworthy authorities consider it to have been composed greatly earlier. In the Talmud there is the mention of a Sepher-Yetzira, a book older, apparently, than the Mishna itself. If this is the same work as that now under consideration, it must be referred to the first, or at latest the second, century of Christianity. The language and style of the book are in accordance with this notion, being those of the Apostolic age; and though there are passages suggesting a later date than this, scholars are inclined to coincide in the view of M. Adolph. Francke,[258] that the book belongs to the Apostolic age.

BOOK OF ZOHAR

The Sepher-Zohar, Book of Light,[259] is of the more importance, because it is accounted the code and text-book of the theological system, as adopted by the Chasidim. It takes the form of a commentary on the Mosaic Books, and is extremely mystical and full of allegory. Its contents are thus described by Surenhusius: 'Veteris Ecclesiæ judaicæ fundamenta, prout Templo Hierosolymano stante secundo erant, non ex opere Talmudico, vel ab alio quodam auctore antiquo, sed ex Zohare tantum sunt quærenda. Cum in opere Talmudico, leges Ecclesiasticæ, forenses et politicæ exponantur, in Zohare autem loca scripturæ sacræ ad Theologiæ capita reducantur, in quibus de Existentiâ, de Attributis, de Epithetis, ac Nominibus Dei, itemque de Messiâ, de Angelis, tam bonis quam malis, de animâ humanâ, ejusdemque origine ac statu, atque, ut uno verbo dicam, de cognitione Dei nostri per Messiam genuinum Filium, agitur.'

Its authorship and date are even more a matter of dispute than those of the Yetzira. It is said by many to be the composition of Simeon Jochaides (Simeon ben Yochai), who is believed to have lived somewhere about the time of our Lord. Others, though they do not consider Simeon to be the actual author, yet are of opinion that it was written by one of his scholars, who embodied in it his master's teaching. The language in which it is written is that of the Palestinian Jews in the times immediately preceding the composition of the Talmud. 'The ideas and expressions also,' writes Etheridge, 'belong to that date.' It would be possible, however, perhaps not very difficult, to simulate that style, if it was the object of the composer to pass it off as the production of an early age; and it is difficult to believe that some of the contents of the book could be the work of any Jew of the date assigned. M. Francke's opinion here also is the safest to follow. He places it in the seventh century. The notion, however, that the Zohar is simply the composition of Moses de Léon, fully six hundred years afterwards, finds supporters even at the present day.

It is in form, as has already been intimated, a commentary on the Pentateuch; but in reality a heterogeneous mass of doctrine—the Aristotelian, Neo-Platonic, and Rabbinical conceptions being inextricably blended together. It professes to reveal great mysteries; but the revelation is conveyed in language so enigmatical and obscure that it is often difficult to arrive at any definite meaning. It recognises God as the Infinite, having no beginning, and no end of existence; and declares that He has revealed Himself under ten forms, or rather emanations, to which the Zohar gives the name of Sephiroth. These ten are Transcendency (the crown), Wisdom, Knowledge, Mercy, Justice, Beauty, Triumph, Glory, Basis, Dominion. In all these representations the Triune character of the Godhead is exhibited. [260] Hence, in the confession of faith adopted by the Zoharites, as the followers of Jacob Frank and others were called, the doctrine of the Blessed Trinity, as held by the Church Catholic, was distinctly professed.

FOOTNOTES:

[254] This story may, or may not, be historical; but any way it illustrates the use of the Massoretic points.

[255] The Massorites were an inferior description of Scribes, whose profession it was to write out copies of the Hebrew Scriptures; also to teach the people the true readings, as well as to comment on them. They called their work 'Massora,' or tradition, because they believed that God gave the Law on Sinai, imparting to Moses, at the same time, the true interpretation.

[256] Graetz says of the Cabbala, that it is a fungous growth, which since the thirteenth century has crept over the body of the Law.

[257] The Talmud is said to have been publicly burnt in Podolia, a.d. 1755, by some Sabbathain Cabbalists. On

the other side, the Rabbinical Talmudists have repeatedly condemned the Cabbalism of the Chasidim.

[258] *La Cabbale*, par Adolph. Francke, Paris, 1843; a work of extensive research and profound learning.

[259] Daniel xii. 3. The word is there rendered by our translators, as 'brightness.'

[260] It is proper to remark that Jewish controversialists deny the existence of Trinitarian doctrine in the Book of Zohar. On the contrary, they affirm that they were wont to twit the Cabbalists with 'believing in ten gods, whereas (said they) even the Christians believed in only three.'

APPENDIX IV
THE ATTEMPT UNDER JULIAN
TO REBUILD THE TEMPLE

Grave doubts have been advanced, by one writer or another, of what may be called the ancient belief on this subject. It has been questioned: I. Whether the attempt to rebuild the Temple ever was really made; and II. whether, allowing the work to have been begun and interrupted, its interruption was not due to natural causes only.

I. It is argued, chiefly by Lardner,[261] that Julian did no more than project such an undertaking, which he never attempted to carry into effect. In his letter addressed to the Jewish people, he tells them, '*if* he returned from his Persian expedition, he would rebuild and inhabit with them the holy city of Jerusalem.' But, as he never returned, Lardner argues that he never made the promised attempt. The same appears to be the tradition of the Jews.[262] Thus, David Gans, in the fifteenth century, writes, 'The work was prevented from being accomplished, *for* Julian never returned, but perished in the Persian War;' and similarly Cassel: 'He made preparations for restoring the Temple, but, after a brief reign, fell in battle.' A passage from one of Julian's orations is, further, quoted by Lardner, in which he says that, 'he conceived the design of rebuilding the Temple.' But, as he does not add that he executed it, Lardner reasons that he probably did not.

It is almost needless to say that these arguments carry very little weight. The reader should note that Julian did not promise to rebuild the *Temple*, on his return from Persia, but *Jerusalem*. As that city was then standing, his meaning must have been, that he would restore it to its pristine magnificence. This would be a long and costly work, which might well require his personal presence. But he might commit the rebuilding of the Temple, the design of which was well known, to a deputy—an instalment, so to speak, of the greater work to follow. Nor can it be reasonably argued, that, because a man does not say that he put in force a design, *therefore* he *did* not put it in force. [263]

Whatever weight Lardner's reasoning might carry is lost altogether, when we take into consideration the testimony of the contemporaneous historians, and those of the age immediately following. The first include Gregory Nazianzen, Bishop of Constantinople, John Chrysostom, Cyril of Jerusalem, Ambrose, and Ammianus Marcellinus; the second, Socrates, Sozomen, and Theodoret. All these record the main facts, viz., the repeated bursting forth of the fire, until the work was abandoned from the impossibility of persisting. Each adds some minor details, which do not affect the credibility of the occurrence itself.[264] The most important witness is Ammianus Marcellinus, a heathen and a personal friend of the Emperor. It will be better to give his account of the matter in his own words. 'The Emperor was meditating,' he writes,[265] 'the restoration, at an unlimited expense, of the Jewish Temple, and had committed the care of the matter to Alypius of Antioch. When, then, Alypius was vigorously prosecuting the work, and the governor of the province was rendering him his help, frightful balls of fire breaking forth with continued outbursts near the foundations, again and again consumed the workmen, and rendered it impossible to approach the spot; and in this manner the element more obstinately (*i.e.*, more obstinately than even the pertinacious persistence of the workmen) driving them away, the attempt was abandoned.'

In the face of evidence like this, he must be a hardy advocate who would maintain that the occurrence never took place.

But it may be contended that although it did take place, there was nothing in it of a miraculous character. It may be alleged,—

(1) That there was simply an earthquake, to which the whole was due.

(2) That there may have been an explosion of foul air, caused by the sudden opening of the vaults under the Temple. These had long been closed, and the noxious vapours, coming into contact with the workmen's fires, exploded.

(3) That it is improbable that such a miracle *would* be worked, there being nothing in the rebuilding of the Temple which *called for* a miracle. Our Lord, no doubt, had declared that the Temple should be utterly destroyed, but not that it should never be rebuilt. Nor had Daniel (rightly understood), or any other prophet, ever said so.

(4) That the age in which the miracle is related to have taken place is one in which miracles are spoken of as having been of almost daily occurrence— some of them frivolous and childish to the last degree. In these no reasonable man can place any faith; and there is nothing to separate this miracle from them.

Let us consider these objections.

1. Earthquakes have always been of common occurrence in Palestine. Nor is it denied that an earthquake took place on the present occasion. But a simple earthquake will not account for the bursting forth of the fiery balls, *as often as the labourers attempted to resume the work*. No other earthquake ever exhibited these phenomena.

2. This explanation was, I believe, unknown to Warburton, Basnage, Lardner, or Gibbon. It appears to have been first suggested in a German magazine,[266] by the celebrated Michaelis, in the latter half of the eighteenth century. But, on inquiry, it appears more ingenious than probable. Who knows that the caverns under the Temple *had* been hermetically sealed for a long time previously to Julian's attempt? They were constantly opened at other times (as the story told by Benjamin of Tudela evidences), and no such result followed. The present was but one out of many occasions when foundations had been dug and buildings erected in the same spot; but without any explosion or fiery outburst. How was it that Solomon's workmen, and Zorobabel's, and Adrian's, and I know not how many more— how was it that they escaped the fatal injuries that befell those of Julian?

Again, the phenomena related by Marcellinus and others do not accord with the idea of an explosion of mephitic gases. These ignite instantaneously, and burn till exhausted. They could not be described by any writer as '*balls* of fire' breaking forth with continual outbursts, as often as the labourers attempted to resume the work. It is also evident that the fire did not break forth the moment the ground was opened, but only when the whole foundation had been laid and the masons had begun to build; for Chrysostom says that some of the stones already laid were thrown down.

3. In dealing with this objection, we enter on new and more difficult ground. It may be true, and I incline to believe it is so, that the truth of Holy Writ was not, so to speak, imperilled by this enterprise. If it had succeeded, I do not see that any saying of Inspiration would have been thereby contravened.[267] But such an occurrence would surely have been at variance with the Divine purpose in setting up the Christian Church. Type and shadow were to vanish when the reality and the substance came. The rebuilding of the Jewish Temple would have been an unmeaning renewal of them. Further, such strange anomalies as the reconstruction of the Holy of Holies, with its veil unrent, and the renewal of the Temple sacrifices, foreshadowing an event long past, would have disturbed the faith of large numbers of professing members of the Church, as well as deterred equally large numbers from entering its pale. It is a difficult—it may be thought a presumptuous—thing to attempt determining what would be a sufficient reason for expecting a miracle. But if there ever has been an instance in the history of the Christian Church when a miracle was, so to speak, demanded,

it was the one we have under consideration. Almighty God had been directly challenged by the supreme human ruler of the earth, and in the sight of all Christendom, to show the right. Do we wonder that, as at Mount Carmel, He answered by fire?

4. These considerations make it easy to deal with the last of the four objections. It may freely be granted that the age of Julian was signalized by the endless recurrence of reported miracles—most of which must be regarded with grave suspicion, while many others are wholly unworthy of credit. Thus Gregory relates of Julian, that one day when he was sacrificing, the entrails of the victim were found to be impressed with the emblem of a cross within a circle.[268] On another occasion, when he attempted to build a heathen temple over the spot where a Christian had been buried, it fell down again as soon as it was put up.[269] These are two instances, out of many, of the idle tales current in that day. If the occurrence we have now under consideration is to be classed with these, no one could wonder at the unwillingness of men to lend it credit. But it stands entirely apart from them. It was not worked at the command or through the entreaty of any man. It was not manifested to prove the truth of any disputed dogma, or the sanctity of any theological leader, or the orthodoxy of any party in the Church. It was wrought by the finger of God directly and visibly; and, unless we are prepared to affirm that since the Apostolic age He has never openly interfered in the affairs of men, we may reasonably believe that He interfered here.

FOOTNOTES:

[261] Lardner, V. iii. p. 603 ff.

[262] Cassel, I. § 53. Other Jewish writers, as Jost, admit the occurrence, but deny the miracle.

[263] Lardner also insists much on the silence of Jerome, Prudentius, and Orosius. If facts of history are to be doubted because some historians of the time do not mention them how many would remain which could be regarded as certain?

[264] Thus, Gregory says that the doors of a church were miraculously closed against the fugitives, and a fiery flame issuing from it destroyed them; that a circle and cross of fire were visible in the heavens, and crosses of fire seen on the garments of the spectators. Chrysostom states that the workmen had dug out the foundation, and begun to build, when the flames burst forth. Socrates, that the building tools

and implements were consumed by fire, and were a whole day burning, He adds, what is important, that the earthquake occurred during the night, and the fires broke out on the following day. Theodoret says that the earthquake threw down some of the stones of the newly laid foundations, and shook some of the excavated earth back into the hole out of which it had been dug. Chrysostom confirms him in this.

[265] Ammian. Marcellin. XXIII. 1. It has been suggested that he took his account without inquiry from Christian writers. So Gibbon, ch. XXXIII. But that a heathen historian and devoted friend of Julian should in this manner have recorded what was at once unfavourable to his creed and painful to his feelings as a friend, is too improbable to need refutation.

[266] *Magazin von Lichtenberg.* Quoted by the editor of Ammian. Marcell. in his notes.

[267] Warburton argues that not only did our Lord never declare that the Jewish Temple should not be rebuilt, but that He even implied that it would be, when He said (St. Luke xxi. 24), 'Jerusalem shall be trodden down of the Gentiles, *until* the times of the Gentiles be fulfilled.' But this is to mistake the meaning of the Greek phrase Ἄχρις οὗ, ἕως οὗ. These denote a state of things up to a given point, but determine nothing as to what will follow. See Chrysostom on St. Matt. i. 25 etc.

[268] Greg. Naz. Orat. III.

[269] Chrysost. in Matth. Hom. IV.

APPENDIX V
THE BLOOD ACCUSATIONS

Among the many accusations which have been advanced against the Jews, there are three, which may be distinguished from the others as 'Blood Accusations,' and which have been the causes of terrible suffering to them. The first of these is the charge of crucifying boys, in parody of the Saviour's death upon the cross; the second, that of using Christian blood in the preparation of the Paschal cakes; the third, that of possessing themselves, by underhand means, of the consecrated Host, for the purpose of insulting and stabbing it. It might seem that this last was not a *blood* accusation. But, as it was believed that they cut and pierced the wafer, as being the very body of the Lord, which indeed bled like any human body under their knives, it may be classed with the other two. The first is the most ancient, and the one which has been most pertinaciously adhered to; though the other two have been continually repeated and accredited. Our present object is to inquire when these charges were first made, and what could have given rise to them.

As regards the time and origin of the notion respecting their crucifixion of boys, I have at p. 73 suggested the probable source of that accusation. Of all the Jewish feasts, the most mirthful, or rather the most riotous, was the Feast of Purim; of which it was said that 'the Jews were wont to drink, until they could not distinguish between the blessings pronounced on Mordecai and the curses imprecated on Haman.' At this feast, in the earlier centuries of Christianity, it was customary to introduce the effigy of Haman suspended on his gibbet; and the resemblance of this figure to a crucified malefactor soon engaged the notice of the Jews. Hence jests and innuendos against our Blessed Lord came to be a common topic among the revellers; on which ground the Jews were forbidden by the Christian emperors to celebrate this feast. Nor did the Jews confine their insolence to words. On one occasion, at Inmestar, they seized a Christian youth, whom they fastened to Haman's gibbet, and scourged so mercilessly that he died under their hands. This, of course, provoked a fierce outburst of indignation and horror; and we can well understand that the tradition of the outrage would spread far and endure for many generations.

The second accusation—that of mixing Christian blood with the Passover cakes, or, as some said, with the Paschal sacrifice itself, does not appear to have been advanced until some time in the 13th century, though the exact date cannot be determined. Now, it is at least remarkable in connection with this charge, that it was first made just about the time when the doctrine of Transubstantiation was beginning to take forcible hold on men's minds. [270] That was declared for the first time to be a doctrine of the Catholic faith, by a Lateran Council a.d. 1215. According to that belief, the eucharistic wafer became, after consecration, the actual body and blood of the Lord, so that men actually ate His flesh and drank His blood. It may be assumed as tolerably certain that the Jews would mock and deride this doctrine; which great numbers of pious Christians found themselves unable to accept. Even if the Jews did not openly satirize the Christians who upheld this extravagant conception, their opinion about it would be notorious enough; nor could the knowledge of what the Jews thought about it fail to exasperate still further the bitterness with which the extreme zealots of Ultramontanism already regarded them. It was an easy and obvious addition to the old charge of crucifying a Christian in mockery of the Saviour's passion, to say that the Jews further mixed the blood of their victim with the Paschal bread, in order to deride the holy rite whereby Christians became partakers of His very body and blood.

The Jews themselves allege other reasons for the circulation of this slander. They declare the charge to have been first made in the earliest ages of the Church, and to have been levelled, nominally indeed at the Jews, but really at the Christians. A vague rumour of the words spoken by Jesus at the Paschal Supper, when He delivered the cup to the Apostles, 'This is My blood,' had spread among the heathen, and given the idea that the Christians actually drank human blood at their religious celebrations. It is true that the authors of these accusations attribute the offence to the Israelites; but (say the Jews, and so far certainly truly) the earlier heathen writers continually confound the Christians with Jews, regarding the former as simply an heretical Jewish sect. Further, it is alleged that the calumny derived some support from the known practice of certain heretical Christian sects, notably the Cataphrygians, who mixed with the consecrated bread the blood of infants, which they extracted from them by puncturing a vein. This, however, is nothing more than a plausible theory. Granting that such reports gained currency in the first or second century of Christianity, the Christians, against whom they were really circulated, would know their monstrous falsehood, and entirely disregard them. It is impossible to conceive that they would have retorted such a charge on the Jews, or even countenanced its circulation.

Again, it is said that there is an imperative order in the Talmud,[271] that the Jews shall, at the Passover, drink a certain quantity of 'red wine,' and that this 'red wine' was supposed to mean really human blood, though the command was disguised under a metaphor. But independently of the extravagance of such an interpretation of very plain and simple words, the charge made against the Jews was not that of *drinking* Christian blood, but of mixing it with the Passover bread. No one ever supposed that for any of the four cups drunk at the Paschal Feast a cup of human blood was substituted.

If the idea above named has nothing but its likelihood to support it, at all events it has that. And the third charge, brought not long afterwards, of getting surreptitious possession of the consecrated wafer in order to treat it with indignity, tends to strengthen the likelihood. It is alleged that, not content with deriding the doctrine of Transubstantiation, they were eager to insult the body of the Lord itself. They would bribe with a large sum some official to purloin the Host, and hand it over to them—when they would stab it with their knives, and it would bleed, like any human body—they, it was assumed, remaining wholly unmoved by the sight of so tremendous a miracle, nay, only anxious, by multiplied evidence of it, to increase their own condemnation in the sight of Heaven! It is beyond dispute that these alleged marvels were quoted in support of the doctrine of the Corporal Presence in the Eucharist. It is hardly too much to assume that the charges against the Jews were coined—partly, no doubt, in consequence of the bitter hate with which they were regarded, but partly also to establish the certainty of the popular dogma of the day.

I have not thought it necessary to advance any arguments to prove the falsehood of these accusations. No competent tribunal by which they have been tried has ever failed to declare them groundless. Indeed, no person who has the most ordinary acquaintance with the Mosaic ritual, but must be aware, not only of the falsehood, but of the absurdity and the impossibility of the charges. The touch, nay the mere contiguity, of a dead body, according to the Jewish law, rendered all persons in its vicinity unclean, so that they could not partake in, much less celebrate, religious rites until they were purged from the pollution. How then could the blood of a murdered person be used in the consecration of victims and offerings, which its very presence would *ipso facto* desecrate? If nothing short of the most distinct statement on the subject will satisfy some minds, they have even that. The words of Moses, Levit. vii. 26, 27, are, 'Ye shall eat *no manner* of blood' (πᾶν αἷμα σὐκ ἔδεσθε)—no blood, not even of beast or bird, how much less, of man!

FOOTNOTES:

[270] 'These accusations began only 600 years ago,' writes De Virga in the *Shebet Yehuda* published in Amsterdam a.d. 1651. 'They commenced in the reign of Alphonso X. of Castile. In his time there was a priest in Spain who in his sermons declared that the Israelites could not sacrifice their Passover unless they had Christian blood to use in the performance of the rite.'

[271] Hierosolym. Talmudis, Fol. II. 1. 'Quæritur de mensurâ poculorum, quæ ebiberunt ad Pascha, aliaque convivia sacra; et qualitate vini. Præceptum est. ut vino rubido præstat officium. Vinum rubrum requiritur in sacris.' See Lightfoot, *Index Talmud. Hierosolym.* Vol. X. p. 509 of his works.

INDEX

Algiers,

Alkihoran,

All Saints' Day,

Almamon, Caliph, *n.*

Almohades, The,

Almozal,

Alphonso II., King of Naples,

Alphonso IV., King of Portugal,

Alphonso V., King of Portugal, *n.*

Alphonso V., King of Spain,

" VI. " ".

" VII. " ".

" VIII. " ".

" IX. " ".

" X. " " , *n.*

Alphonso XI., King of Spain,

Alroy, El David,

Alsatia,

Alvarez, Father, *n.*

" Garcia,

Al Wathek, Caliph,

Alypius,

Amaria,

Ambivius, Procurator,

Ambrose, Bishop,

Amina,

Ammianus Marcellinus, App. IV.

Amru,

Amsterdam,

Anakia,

Ananus, High Priest, *n.*

"   of Babylon,

Anastasius, Emperor,

Ancona,

Andalusia,

Anencletus II., Pope,

Angoulême,

Anjou, Duke of,

Antioch, *n.*

Antiochus Epiphanes,

"   King of Commagene, *n.*

Antipas, Herod,

Antipatris,

Antonelli, Cardinal,

Antonia, Tower of,

Antoninus, Emperor,

Antwerp,

Appollonius Tyaneus,

Aquitaine,

Arabia,

Arabian Nights,

Aragon,

Arbues D'Avila,

Arch of Titus,

Archelaus,

Arianism,

Arians, *n.*

Aristobulus,

Aristotle,

Arles,

Armleder,

Arnheim,

Arnold, Archbishop, *n.*

Artaxerxes, King,

Asa *or* Asche, Rabbi,

Asaph, St., Bishop (Drummond),

Ascalon,

Ashkenaz, *n.*

Ashkenazim, *n.*, *n.*

Assassins,

Augustus, Emperor,

Aurelian, Emperor,

Aurelius, Emperor,

Austerlitz, Battle of,

Austria,

Averroes,

Avignon,

Avila, Bishop of,

Ayala, Lopes de,

Azores,

Azotus,

B

Baalbek,

Babylon,

Babylonian Schools,

Baechoo,

Bagdad,

Bajazet, Sultan, *n.*

Balavignus,

Balsora,

Bamberg,

Banditono,

Bannister's 'Holy Land,' *n.*

Barabbas (Jew of Malta), *n.*

Barbarini, Cardinal,

Barbary,

Barcelona,

" Cortes at,

Barchochebas,

Barons' War,

Basle, Council at,

Basnage,

Basques, The,

Bassorah,

Bauer, Bruno,

Bavaria,

Bayonne,

Beausobre, *n.*

Belgium,

Belgrade,

Belisarius, *n.*, *n.*

Belmont, Baron de,

Beltran, Bishop,

Benedict XIII., Pope,

" XIV. " .

" the Jew,

Beni Israel, The,

Benjamin of Tudela, *n.*,

Bennefeld,

Berlin,

" Treaty of,

Bernaldes,

Bernard of Clairvaulx, *n.*, *n.*

Bernard the Banker,

" II., King of Spain, (of Transtamara).

" III., King of Spain,

" IV., King of Spain,

Hep, Hep,

Heracleonas, *n.*

Heraclius, Emperor,

Herder, *n.*

Herodias,

Herodion,

Hierax of Alexandria,

Hillel I., II., III., *n.*

Hippicus, Tower of,

Hira,

Hiskiah,

Hochstraten,

Holland,

Holmes, Nathaniel,

Holy Land,

Homberg, Herr, *n.*

Homen Lopes,

Homeritis,

Honorius, Emperor,

Hormisdas, King of Persia,

Hosdai, Rabbi,

Hoshiel, Rabbi,

Hugh of Lincoln,

Huguenots,

Hungary,

Huntingdon,

Huss, John,

Ladislaus I., King of Hungary,

Ladislaus II., King of Hungary,

Lamego, Ruez,

Langton, Archbishop,

Languedoc,

Lara, David,

Lavater,

Leghorn (Livorno),

Leibnitz, *n.*

Leinengen, Landgrave of,

Leo X., Pope,

" Rabbi,

" of Modena,

" the Isaurian, Emperor,

Leonis, Peter,

Leopold I., Emperor,

" Duke,

Lepanto, Battle of,

Lessing, *n., n.*

Levi, Samuel,

" Solomon, Bishop of Burgos,

Lexington, Lord,

Lincoln,

Lipman of Mulhouse,

Lippold, Physician,

Lisbon,

Lithuanians,

Lombard Hall, Oxford,

London,

Loraine,

Maimon, Solomon, *n.*

Maimonides,

Malabar, Jews of, *n.,*

Malach,

Malaga,

Malcho, *n.*

Malesherbes,

Mammæa,

Mamun,

Manasseh (*or* Menasseh) ben Israel, *n.*

Manasseh, Menecier,

Manes or Mani,

Mantenu, Jacob,

Mantua,

Marcian, Emperor,

Marco Polo,

Mariana, Historian,

Maria Theresa,

Marlowe, *n.*

Martel, Charles, *n.*

Martial,

Martin V., Pope,

Martin, Henry,

Martina, *n.*

Martinez, Ferdinand,

Masada, *n.,*

Massorites, , Appendix <u>III.</u>

Master of Jews,

Matthew of Paris,

Matthias, High Priest, *n.,*

Zarephath, *n.*

Zealots,

Zebedee, Pharisee,

Zedekias, Physician,

Zeigler, Rabbi,

Zenobia, Queen of Palmyra,

Zion, Mount,

Zoffingen,

Zohar, Book of, *n.*, Appendix III.

Zonaras,

Zoroaster, *n.*

Zosimus,

Zunz, Leopold,

Zutia, *n.*

Zutphen,